Rec'd
2005

HEAVEN

& W. A. CRISWELL
PAIGE PATTERSON

Minneapolis, MN

Library of Congress Cataloging-in-Publication Data

Criswell, W. A. (Wallie A.), date
    Heaven / W. A. Criswell and Paige Patterson.
      p.   cm.
    ISBN 0-89066-239-8
    1. Heaven. 2. Heaven—Biblical teaching. 3. Heaven—Sermons.
4. Heaven—Poetry. 5. Southern Baptist Convention—Sermons.
6. Baptists—Sermons. 7. Sermons, American. I. Patterson, Paige.
II. Title.
BT846.2.C75 1991   91-20340
236′.24—dc20

Cover illustration copyright © 1991 by Michael Hackett

99 98 97 96 95 94 93
9   8   7   6

This special edition is published with the permission of
Tyndale House Publishers, Inc.; Wheaton, IL 60789.

Once in a very great while,
someone enters your life
whose demeanor is gentle,
whose soul is wholesome,
whose spirit is sweet,
whose very presence is encouraging.
You almost wonder
if that person is not,
in fact, an angel from glory.
Such a person is precious
RUTH RAY HUNT
to whom we, with profound gratitude,
dedicate this book on heaven.
When we think of heaven,
our thoughts are first drawn to our Lord
but then beyond His life
to the lives of His people.
And that heavenly life must be
very much like a wonderful afternoon
of encouragement from and
holy fellowship with Ruth Hunt.
God bless you forever, Ruth,
until we all assemble
before His throne.

CONTENTS

PART ONE
What I Believe about Heaven
by W. A. Criswell

PART TWO
What the Bible Says about Heaven
by Paige Patterson

PART THREE
Great Hymns and Poems about Heaven

ACKNOWLEDGMENTS

To the saints of the First Baptist Church of Dallas, Texas, who patiently and enthusiastically listened to these sermons and sang so many of the hymns, we acknowledge our gratitude. To Wendell Hawley of Tyndale House who envisioned this project, and to Wightman Weese who served as the project editor, to Sherry Poe and Jo Ellen Burch who faithfully typed the manuscripts, and to Dorothy Patterson who painstakingly edited every syllable, we express our thanksgiving and appreciation.

We are grateful also to Rick Hand and Keith Ninomiya, who assisted in research for hymns and poems, and to Ellen R. Thompson, former Professor of Theory and Piano at Wheaton College, Wheaton, Illinois. The hymns and poems in part 3 of this book came from her collection.

W. A. Criswell   *Paige Patterson*

INTRODUCTION

HEAVEN is a place where most people want to reside at the conclusion of this present life. And most folks assume that they will be in heaven. Some years ago when presidential hopefuls crowded to center stage, several pastors and theologians were privileged to be part of a group that queried each of these candidates concerning his perspective and aspiration. Dr. James Kennedy of Coral Ridge Presbyterian Church in Fort Lauderdale, Florida, always asked his now-famous question, "Were you to find yourself standing before the omnipotent God of this universe, what possible reason could you give as a rationale for your admission to heaven?"

The answers were diverse as well as revealing. One candidate replied after only a moment's hesitation, "I would tell him that if he is going to let anyone in, he will have to let me in." Apparently, this man had never thought deeply about the subject, but, nevertheless, he assumed on some casual basis that his destiny in heaven was at least as certain as anyone's could possibly be. His number is legion. As a matter of record, almost all of those who belong to any Christian denomination profess heaven as final destination. Secret organizations such as the Masonic order join with Moslems and others in anticipating some sort of "heavenly" existence.

Popular conceptions of heaven, even among traditional Protestants and free church people who are ostensibly "people of the Book," are often loosely anchored to scriptural moorings at best and frequently owe more to contemporary myth and a sort of sloppy, syrupy sentimentalism than to any clear declaration of Scripture. And sometimes "heavenly images" actually fail to inspire a younger generation. Ideas picturing a kind of celestial "cloud potato," resting eternally in the fluff while strumming a harp and polishing his halo, are unlikely to appeal to an adventuresome eighteen-year-old who in any event has no musical skills. Mention of "eternal worship" in the heavenly domain for those unfamiliar with the real worship of heaven conjures the horrifying spectacle of an eternal eleven o'clock Sunday morning worship service and probably has the virtue of increasing one's efforts to stay alive on this earth just as long as possible.

To exacerbate the situation, the biblical text does abound with references to heaven; yet in the task of interpretation, the painful discovery is that the materials about heaven frequently defy our most strenuous hermeneutical endeavors and ultimately leave us with a plethora of unanswered questions. Nevertheless, the arduous nature of the interpreter's task, the sentimentalism and sometimes mythological cast of modern ideas of heaven should only spur us on to greater vigor.

This volume intends to address some of the questions with which a believer may profitably grapple on the basis of a study of God's revelation of himself and his eternal abode in the Bible. The four sermons included provide examples for the preacher who recognizes the inestimable value of preaching the heavenly promises to inspire hope, witness, and holy living among his parishioners. The section of hymns and poems, spanning much of the Christian era, serves to demonstrate the extent to which the hope and contemplation of heaven have shaped the life of the church in every era.

As the reader engages both the exposition and the sermons

of this volume, he must remember that it is always easier to understand the present than to revisit the past. And if it proves challenging to uncover the past with its deposited and helpful clues, comprehending the future, even through the powerful telescope of biblical prophecy, produces unparalleled difficulties. The analogy to the telescope is a good one. Looking through a telescope we can view "luminaries" in the heavens hidden from the unaided eye. But when we look, we often must say that we certainly see the light, though its precise shape, size, characteristics, etc., may allude us altogether.

My prayer is that this book will help the reader to see the luminary, even if its precise definition awaits a better and more glorious day. Furthermore, my hope is that the reading of these pages will stir up in the reader a renewed hope for "a city whose builder and maker is God."

Paige Patterson
President's Study
The Criswell College
Dallas, Texas

PART ONE
What I Believe about Heaven
W.A. Criswell

CHAPTER 1

What I Believe about Heaven:
The Place

Let not your heart be troubled: ye believe in God, believe also in me.

In my Father's house are many mansions: if it were not so, I would have told you. I go to prepare a place for you.

And if I go and prepare a place for you, I will come again, and receive you unto myself; that where I am, there ye may be also. (John 14:1-3)

We are all profoundly impressed with an everlasting interest in heaven. Our citizenship is in heaven: "For our conversation is in heaven; from whence also we look for the Savior, the Lord Jesus Christ" (Phil. 3:20).

Our names are written in heaven: "Notwithstanding in this rejoice not, that the spirits are subject unto you; but rather rejoice, because your names are written in heaven" (Luke 10:20).

Our treasures are stored in heaven: "But lay up for yourselves treasures in heaven, where neither moth nor rust doth corrupt, and where thieves do not break through nor steal" (Matt. 6:20).

Our eternal home will be in heaven: "In my Father's house are many mansions; if it were not so, I would have told you. I go to prepare a place for you" (John 14:2).

I am a stranger here
Heaven is my home.
Earth is a desert drear
Heaven is my home.
Round me on every hand.
Heaven is my fatherland;
Heaven is my home.

The abode of God is in heaven:

Look down from heaven, and behold from the habitation of thy holiness and of thy glory: where is thy zeal and thy strength, the sounding of thy bowels and of thy mercies toward me? are they restrained? (Isa. 63:15)

In fact, occasionally the very name "heaven" is used as a synonym for God. The prodigal son said to his father, "I will arise and go to my father, and will say unto him, Father, I have sinned against heaven, and before thee" (Luke 15:18).

As the heart and soul of our Christian message, heaven is our hope for life beyond the veil of death.

Poignantly do I remember that one time, as a young pastor of a village church, I attended a meeting of the Green River Baptist Association in the hill country of Kentucky. This convocation of messengers from sixty-five quarter-time churches (these churches had services just once a month) was held outdoors where we sat on split logs under the trees. As the program progressed, somebody stood up and began to sing a song; another joined in; finally, all were standing and singing this song, shaking hands with one another and weeping:

My heavenly home is bright and fair,
And I want to be traveling on.

No harm or death can enter there,
And I want to be traveling on.

Oh, the Lord has been so good to me,
I feel like traveling on.
Until those mansions I can see,
I feel like traveling on.

What Is Heaven Like?

The Bible speaks about the openness of heaven. For example, in Ezekiel 1:1, in John 1:51, in Acts 7:56, in Acts 10:11, the viewer says, "I saw heaven opened." But only in the book of Revelation is there a record of what the viewer actually saw as heaven opened.

Beginning in chapter 4 and continuing in the succeeding chapters of the Apocalypse, John, the sainted apostle of Christ, enters into that glorious realm and describes it for us in vivid detail. The word *heaven* is used fifty-six times in those chapters.

Heaven Is a Place

Twice Jesus calls heaven *topos* (Greek), meaning "a place."

In my Father's house are many mansions: if it were not so, I would have told you. I go to prepare a place for you. And if I go and prepare a place for you, I will come again, and receive you unto myself; that where I am, there ye may be also. (John 14:2-3){xext}

Here heaven is described as a real place. In this same passage Jesus calls heaven *oikos* (Greek), meaning "a house, a dwelling, a home." There are some who say heaven is "a state of mind," "a fancy," "a dream," "an abstraction," "an idea," "wishful thinking," "a figure," "a sentiment." But, the Bible testifies that heaven is as real as the home in which you live and as the city in which you dwell.

The Bible says that Jesus, after His resurrection, was taken up into heaven: "Ye men of Galilee, why stand ye gazing up into heaven? this same Jesus, which is taken up from you into heaven, shall so come in like manner as ye have seen him go into heaven" (Acts 1:11).

Did Jesus go up into a state of mind, into an abstraction? No! Jesus went to a real place, a genuine home, the final and permanent and eternal assembly of God's saints.

Jesus never taught us to say, "Our Father who art in a state of mind or condition." He never said, "I go to prepare an abstraction for you." Ezekiel did not write, "I saw a fanciful dream open unto me." The martyr Stephen did not say, "Behold, I see sentimental figures opened and the Son of Man standing on the right hand of God." These holy men of God declared that Jesus went to a real place called heaven.

Heaven Is a Renewed World Creation

And I saw a new heaven and a new earth: for the first heaven and the first earth were passed away; and there was no more sea. And I John saw the holy city, new Jerusalem, coming down from God out of heaven, prepared as a bride adorned for her husband. (Rev. 21:1-2)

There are two Greek words used in the New Testament for "new"—*neos* and *kainos*. *Neos* is a word used with reference to time. On the other hand, *kainos* refers to quality or kind of character. The latter word, *kainos*, is the only word for "new" used in the book of Revelation. We have a "new [*kainos*] name" (Rev. 2:17; 3:12). We sing a "new [*kainos*] song" (Rev. 5:9;

14:3). We live in a "new [*kainos*] Jerusalem" (Rev. 3:12; 21:2). We possess and enjoy "new [*kainos*] things" (Rev. 21:5). We dwell in a "new [*kainos*] earth," and a "new [*kainos*] heaven" (Rev. 21:1). This word [*kainos*] never refers to annihilation but rather to re-creation and redemption. Matter or substance is indestructible, and there is never a loss of any atom or particle of God's creation.

"One generation passeth away, and another generation cometh: but the earth abideth for ever" (Eccl.1:4). This passage avows that the earth, that is, the substance of the earth, abides forever. In Genesis 1:1-2, the chaotic heaven and the distorted earth are reborn or remade: "In the beginning God created the heaven and the earth. And the earth was without form, and void; and darkness was upon the face of the deep. And the Spirit of God moved upon the face of the waters."

In Genesis chapters 6, 7, and 8, the flood overflowed the earth but did not annihilate it. Likewise, in 2 Peter 3:10-13, the world is purified by fire, but it is not wiped out of existence. Paul uses this same word (*kainos*) to refer to spiritual regeneration: "Therefore if any man be in Christ, he is a new [*kainos*] creature: old things are passed away; behold, all things are become new [*kainos*]" (2 Cor. 5:17).

Consider also these references:

> For in Christ Jesus neither circumcision availeth any thing, nor uncircumcision, but a new creature. (Gal. 6:15)

> Having abolished in his flesh the enmity, even the law of commandments contained in ordinances; for to make in himself of twain one new man, so making peace. (Eph. 2:15)

> And that ye put on the new man, which after God is created in righteousness and true holiness. (Eph. 4:24)

In these verses, Paul referred to those of us who have been saved and regenerated. We do become a new people. Though we are in the same body and possessed of the same soul, we are regenerated and transformed. This transformation makes us like Jesus; we have the same body and soul, but our hearts and lives have been transfigured through the process of regeneration. There is no loss of continuity or identity. You will be you, and I shall be I, and we shall be we—the same persons. Thus, our world will be made new (*kainos*), purged from moral and physical imperfections in order to become the eternal abode of Christ's living saints.

Our New Home in Heaven
Is Located in a Beautiful City

Not only is heaven a real place, and not only is this present world made new, but also we shall have a new home located in a new and beautiful city. Cities will always rise and dominate a land. For example, Paris is France; Rome is Italy; London is England; Jerusalem is Israel. You do not think of any of these countries without associating with that country its most famous city. John was a Galilean. He was not a city dweller; he lived in the countryside, fertile with fruits and flowers. But the view he saw of the life that is yet to be was not in a lovely but lonely Garden of Eden but rather in a vast, interminable city—the New Jerusalem.

God sets before us the life of a city thronging with people. Zechariah 8:5 describes the city as one with boys and girls playing in her streets. God said, "It is not good that the man should be alone" (Gen. 2:18). Our happiness, by God's design, depends upon others. Paul wrote, "For none of us liveth to himself, and no man dieth to himself" (Rom. 14:7). We are placed in families, in groups, in churches, in towns, in cities. In this great city, the New Jerusalem, we shall have an eternity in which to see, know, enjoy, and get acquainted with each other.

The revelation of a City of God goes back to Abraham. "For he [Abraham] looked for a city which hath foundations, whose builder and maker is God" (Heb. 11:10). This city was a strong contrast to the temporary tent in which Abraham dwelt, and that city became the prayerful desire and hope of those pilgrim souls who lived in that ancient day.

> And truly, if they had been mindful of that country from whence they came out, they might have had opportunity to have returned. But now they desire a better country, that is, a heavenly: wherefore God is not ashamed to be called their God: for he hath prepared for them a city. (Heb. 11:15-16)

How amazing that those pilgrims of that ancient day looked forward to a beautiful city of God! This heavenly city is the workmanship of Christ Himself. Jesus was a carpenter; He was a builder. He announced that He was going away to prepare for us mansions for our eternal home.

> Let not your heart be troubled: ye believe in God, believe also in me. In my Father's house are many mansions: if it were not so, I would have told you. I go to prepare a place for you. And if I go and prepare a place for you, I will come again, and receive you unto myself; that where I am, there ye may be also. And whither I go ye know, and the way ye know. (John 14:1-4)

What a wonder those mansions, the work of His hands, must be! In only six days the Lord created a universe. Yet He has already been two thousand years in the preparation of the homes in heaven where we are going to live throughout eternity.

The Lord God loves detail: look at the wings of a butterfly. The Lord God loves color: look at a rainbow, a sunset, the blue of the azure sky. The Lord God loves beauty: behold the jeweled foundations of the New Jerusalem. The Lord God loves music: listen to the orchestras of heaven and their new songs. The Lord God loves a garden: walk through the new Paradise (*paradise* is a Persian loan word meaning "garden") with its rivers and its tree of life.

We are invited in Revelation chapters 21 and 22 to share in a panoramic view of our eternal home—the city itself in all of its glory. First, John described the city from the outside. It is measured—a solid cube of golden construction—one thousand five hundred miles up, down, and across (Rev. 21:15-17). It is as large as from the farthest point of Maine to the farthest tip of Florida. It is as large as from the Atlantic Ocean to the Rocky Mountains. It is as large as all western Europe and one half of Russia. Each street is one half the length of the diameter of the earth. The levels arise one mile above the other, equaling eight million miles of beautiful avenues. The three gates upon the twelve jeweled foundations proclaim security and accessibility from all parts of the earth (Rev. 21:14). The entire city of splendor proclaims God's covenant relationship with the bride of the Lamb—His people Israel and His redeemed Church.

After John unveils his detailed description of the outside of this magnificent city, he takes us inside. Oh, what a glory! As one walks those beautiful avenues, two things are not present. First, there is no sun and no moon. The city is illuminated by the presence of God himself (Rev. 21:23). He is the source of uncreated light.

Once in a while you see this phenomenon in the stories of the Bible. When Moses came down from the mountain and the presence of God, his face shown, reflecting the glory of the light of God. When the Lord Jesus was transfigured, his face, his raiment, his bodily form became iridescent, the uncreated light of the presence of God. When Paul was on his way to Damascus to haul into prison those who called upon the name of Jesus, he met the Lord in the way and was blinded by the glory of that light. That is the light of heaven—uncreated. In heaven, we shall see God's face and live.

Second, there is no temple there (Rev. 21:22). The book of Revelation is written by a man who lived in a day in which great cities were full of beautiful temples. Herod's temple was in Jerusalem. The temple of Athena was on the Acropolis in Athens. The temple of Artemis or Diana, one of the great wonders of the world, was located in Ephesus. But here in the new Jerusalem, in the home where the redeemed shall live, a great temple is not needed because the redeemed shall live in the presence of God himself, and they shall look directly into the face of the Almighty with no veil to separate them from him.

Is all this a dream, a fancy, a capricious delusion, wishful thinking? No! God himself reveals to us the reality of our heavenly home.

> But as it is written, Eye hath not seen, nor ear heard, neither have entered into the heart of man, the things which God hath prepared for them that love him. But God hath revealed them unto us by his Spirit: for the Spirit searcheth all things, yea, the deep things of God. (1 Cor. 2:9-10)

This glorious future abode becomes real to those who have found hope in Jesus. The longing in the hearts of the redeemed becomes a faithful revelation and reality in the promise and in the omnipotence of God. When one is saved, the persuasion of the reality of a heavenly home is born in him the minute he opens his heart to the faith, hope, love, and grace of the Lord Jesus. Heaven—not earth—is the home of the redeemed. The Israelites wandered in the desert for forty years before they approached the Promised Land and looked into Canaan. What lay between the wandering and the Promised Land? The waters of the Jordan—the symbol of death—lay between. And to go into our Promised Land, our heavenly home, we—the redeemed—must go through the waters of death.

Isaac Watts, one of the greatest Christian hymn writers of all the ages, in the seventeenth century wrote a hymn about the river of death, i.e., the Jordan River, that separates us from the new city of Jerusalem.

There is a land of pure delight,
Where saints immortal reign;
Infinite day excludes the night
And pleasures banish pain.

There everlasting spring abides
And never withering flower
Death, *like a narrow sea, divides*
This heavenly land from ours.

Sweet fields beyond the swelling flood
Stand dressed in living green
So to the Jews old Canaan stood
While Jordan rolled between.

But timerous mortals start and shrink
To cross this narrow sea [death]
And linger shivering on the brink
In fear to launch away.

Oh, could we make our doubts remove
Those gloomy doubts that rise,
And see the Canaan that we love
With unbeclouded eyes.

Could we but climb where Moses stood
And view the landscape ore,
Not Jordan's stream, nor death's cold flood
Should fright us from the shore.

Because of our fallen natures we dread death. Actually, however, death is just a stream that divides us from our home in heaven. That is why Paul so triumphantly wrote, "Oh, death where is thy sting? Oh, grave where is thy victory? But thanks be to God which giveth us the victory through our Lord Jesus Christ" (1 Cor. 15:55, 57).

That is what God has purposed for us—that better place beyond the river of Jordan, beyond the veil of death. We will be going home. Oh, blessed be the name of our Lord!

Heaven at last! I've reached the harbor
For whose calm I long have prayed.
Filled with awe, I gaze and wonder
At the things my Lord hath made.

Hark! I hear the angels singing,
Morning breaks, the night is past.
And the heavenly bells are ringing,
Welcome, pilgrim—home at last!

CHAPTER 2
What I Believe about Heaven:
The People

After this I beheld, and lo, a great multitude, which no man could number, of all nations, and kindreds, and people, and tongues, stood before the throne, and before the Lamb, clothed with white robes, and palms in their hands; And cried with a loud voice, saying, Salvation to our God which sitteth upon the throne, and unto the Lamb. And all the angels stood round about the throne, and about the elders and the four beasts, and fell before the throne on their faces, and worshiped God, Saying, Amen: Blessing, and glory, and wisdom, and thanksgiving, and honour, and power, and might, be unto our God for ever and ever. Amen. And one of the elders answered, saying unto me, What are these which are arrayed in white robes? and whence came they? And I said unto him, Sir, thou knowest, And he said to me, These are they which came out of great tribulation, and have washed their robes, and made them white in the blood of the Lamb. Therefore are they before the throne of God, and serve him day and night in his temple: and he that sitteth on the throne shall dwell among them. They shall hunger no more, neither thirst any more; neither shall the sun light on them, nor any heat. For the Lamb which is in the midst of the throne shall feed them, and shall lead them unto living fountains of waters: and God shall wipe away all tears from their eyes. (Rev. 7:9-17)

Angels Will Be in Heaven

The word *heaven* occurs 559 times in the Bible, and angels are constantly identified as being in heaven. When we arrive there, the first overwhelming scene we shall behold is that of those multitudes of angels.

> But ye are come unto mount Zion, and unto the city of the living God, the heavenly Jerusalem, and to an innumerable company of angels. (Heb. 12:22)

> And I beheld, and I heard the voice of many angels round about the throne and the beasts and the elders: and the number of them was ten thousand times ten thousand, and thousands of thousands. (Rev. 5:11)

Many times in the Bible angels are presented in multitudinous numbers: "And suddenly there was with the angel a multitude of the heavenly host" (Luke 2:13).

The Lord told Simon Peter to put up his sword. "Thinkest thou that I cannot now pray to my Father, and he shall presently give me more than twelve legions [seventy-two thousand] of angels?" (Matt. 26:53).

Angels are people; they are created by God. They had a beginning of existence just as we.

> Praise ye the Lord. Praise ye the Lord from the heavens: praise him in the heights. Praise ye him, all his angels: praise ye him, all his hosts. Let them praise the name of the Lord: for he commanded, and they were created. (Ps. 148:1-2, 5)

Angels have personality and the basic capacity to have fellowship with God in contradistinction to the animal and the inanimate world. They have intelligence. They seek to learn just as we do. They do not know the time of the return of Christ. "But of that day and hour knoweth no man, no, not the angels of heaven, but my Father only" (Matt. 24:36). They desire and are interested in the whole plan of salvation and in our ultimate victory in the Lord.

> Of which salvation the prophets have inquired and searched diligently, who prophesied of the grace that should come unto you: Searching what, or what manner of time the Spirit of Christ which was in them did signify, when it testified beforehand the sufferings of Christ, and the glory that should follow. Unto whom it was revealed, that not unto themselves, but unto us they did minister the things, which are now reported unto you by them that have preached the gospel unto you with the Holy Ghost sent down from heaven; which things the angels desire to look into. (1 Pet. 1:10-12)

They have emotions; they respond and have feelings just as we do. They rejoice; they were filled with gladness at God's creation of the world. They watched the work of creation: "When the morning stars sang together, and all the sons of God shouted for joy" (Job 38:7).

They bowed in reverence before God: "And one cried unto another, and said, Holy, holy, holy, is the Lord of hosts: the whole earth is full of his glory" (Isa. 6:3). "And again, when he bringeth in the first begotten into the world, he saith, And let all the angels of God worship him" (Heb. 1:6).

They praised God in exaltation at the birth of Christ: "And suddenly there was with the angel a multitude of the heavenly host praising God" (Luke 2:13).

In their presence joy resounds in heaven over one sinner who gives his heart to Jesus. Angels are as we are. They have moral sensitivities; they have the power of choice and discernment.

One third of their number chose to follow Satan: "And his tail drew the third part of the stars of heaven, and did cast them to the earth: and the dragon stood before the woman which was ready to be delivered, for to devour her child as soon as it was born" (Rev. 12:4).

These rebellious angels became forever confirmed in evil doing:

> God spared not the angels that sinned, but cast them down to hell, and delivered them into chains of darkness, to be reserved unto judgment (2 Pet. 2:4).

> And the angels which kept not their first estate, but left their own habitation, he hath reserved in everlasting chains under darkness unto the judgment of the great day. (Jude 6)

On the other hand, the two thirds of their number who chose to follow Christ are forever confirmed in their salvation and, just as we, shall be in heaven, nevermore to be tempted to fall, to err, to sin.

We shall be as the angels in heaven: "For in the resurrection they neither marry, nor are given in marriage, but are as the angels of God in heaven" (Matt. 22:30).

As with the angels in heaven, we shall be confirmed in the service of God forever and ever. Where God is, angels are and we are. If we and the angels are not there, God is not there. They and we are always together and in multitudinous ranks. In the book of the Revelation we see God in heaven as in no other book in the Bible, and there angels appear more frequently than in all the other books of the Bible combined.

Angels have names and are given distinct assignments just as we are. The angel named Michael (meaning "who is like God") is called an archangel (Jude 9). He is called a chief prince and a great prince in Daniel (Dan. 10:13, 21; 12:1). He is God's champion in battle. Always wherever Michael appears, he is leading the forces of God against evil (see Dan. 10; Rev. 12).

Another angel named Gabriel (meaning "the mighty one of God") is God's messenger. He always appears in that same assignment. He was God's messenger to Daniel (Dan. 8:15-27), to Zechariah (Luke 1:11-20), and to Mary (Luke 1:26-38).

Angels are not all alike. They belong to separate orders; they differ just as we do. Some are called cherubim (the plural of a Hebrew word is indicated by the suffix *-im*). The first reference to cherubim is found in Genesis 3:24. In Exodus 25:17-22, the cherubim, with their wings touching, are above the mercy seat. They are upon the tapestry woven in the veil, and they are upon the wall of Solomon's temple.

Some angels are seraphim (the plural of seraph), meaning "the burning ones." The seraphim are consumed, that is, they burn with their devotion for the Lord. An archangel is numbered among the chief princes of heaven, and others are guardian angels. When a little baby is born into this world, an angel that beholds the face of our heavenly Father is assigned to the child: "Take heed that ye despise not one of these little ones; for I say unto you, That in heaven their angels do always behold the face of my Father which is in heaven" (Matt. 18:10).

An angel guided the holy family:

> And when they were departed, behold, the angel of
> the Lord appeareth to Joseph in a dream, saying, Arise,
> and take the young child and his mother, and flee into
> Egypt, and be thou there until I bring thee word: for
> Herod will seek the young child to destroy him. When
> he arose, he took the young child and his mother by
> night, and departed into Egypt. (Matt. 2:13-14)

An angel comforted and ministered to Christ in the hour of His tragic Gethsemane: "And there appeared an angel unto him from heaven, strengthening him" (Luke 22:43).

An angel is assigned to watch over you, and he lovingly cares for you. Angels have been given many varied and distinct assignments. An angel opened the prison doors for the apostles: "But the angel of the Lord by night opened the prison doors, and brought them forth" (Acts 5:19).

One directed Philip in Gaza: "And the angel of the Lord spake unto Philip, saying, Arise, and go toward the south unto the way that goeth down from Jerusalem unto Gaza, which is desert" (Acts 8:26).

Another spoke to Cornelius of Caesarea: "He saw in a vision evidently about the ninth hour of the day an angel of God coming in to him (Acts 10:3).

One delivered Peter from the hand of Herod Agrippa.

And when Herod would have brought him forth, the same night Peter was sleeping between two soldiers, bound with two chains: and the keepers before the door kept the prison. And, behold, the angel of the Lord came upon him, and a light shined in the prison: and he smote Peter on the side, and raised him up, saying, Arise up quickly. And his chains fell off from his hands. And the angel said unto him, Gird thyself, and bind on thy sandals. And so he did. And he saith unto him, Cast thy garment about thee, and follow me. (Acts 12:6-8)

Another stood by Paul in the storm of the Mediterranean: "For there stood by me this night the angel of God, whose I am, and whom I serve" (Acts 27:23).

Have you ever felt that somebody was standing by you during a great trial or testing? God's angel also watches over you.

In the first sentence of the book of Revelation, an angel is the messenger who signified: "The Revelation of Jesus Christ, which God gave unto him, to shew unto his servants things which must shortly come to pass; and he sent and signified it by his angel unto his servant John" (Rev. 1:1).

Though the word is pronounced "sig-ni-fied," its meaning is better understood if it is pronounced "sign-i-fied." That is the purpose of the Apocalypse. An angel signifies (or "sign-i-fies") to John by figure and drama all the course of human history and its consummation. An angel accompanies John as he passes through the scenes of the Apocalypse; an angel executes the fearful judgments of God; an angel reveals to John the glories of the Holy City, the New Jerusalem.

Saved Loved Ones Will Be in Heaven

When we arrive in heaven, not only will the angels of God be there, but also these saints of the Lord who have found refuge in Him will dwell in this glorious place.

An old man was testifying at church on a Wednesday night. He said that as a little boy he pictured heaven as a beautiful city with high walls and domes and stories and a host of white-robed angels and a vast multitude, none of whom he knew. Then as the days passed, his little brother died. Then he said, "I thought about heaven as a great city with walls and turrets and towers and domes and white-robed angels and a vast multitude whom I did not know, as well as one little face I did know—my little brother." Then the old man testified that as the years passed his mother died, his father died, his wife died, his children died. All of the family was gone, and he alone was left. He said, "Now when I think of heaven, I never think of it in terms of high walls and jasper palaces and white-robed angels. I think of it as the dwelling place of my loved ones."

We sing this beautiful song:

I'll sing you a song of that beautiful land,
Far away home of the soul.
Where no storms ever beat on the glittering strand,
While the years of eternity roll.

Oh, how sweet it will be in that beautiful land,
So free from all sorrow and pain.
With songs on our lips and with hearts in our hands,
To greet one another again.

As a teenager in a country church, I conducted my first funeral. I went to a poor tenant's home and watched a little baby die of terrible convulsions. After the service at the little country church, the family and friends put the little casket on a flat-bedded truck. Next to me in my car sat the mother and beside her the father. As that truck pulled out, the mother began to cry piteously, and the father put his arm around her and said, "Sweet, don't cry, our baby is in the arms of Jesus, and He will take care of him. He will keep our child safely, and someday, darling, He will give our baby back to us again." That was my first funeral. What a comfort we as believers have in the promise that someday we will be reunited with those whom we love in Christ. This hope is incomparably sweet and dear beyond words to describe it.

When a believer dies, he goes to Paradise. An angel carries the beggar into Abraham's bosom, another name for Paradise. "And it came to pass, that the beggar died, and was carried by the angels into Abraham's bosom: the rich man also died, and was buried" (Luke 16:22). In Luke 23:43, the Lord says to the repentant thief, "Today [*semeron*, "this day"] thou shalt be with me in Paradise." And in the afternoon that thief was walking the streets of glory with the Lord. Our names are written in heaven: "Notwithstanding in this rejoice not, that the spirits are subject unto you; but rather rejoice, because your names are written in heaven" (Luke 10:20).

Paul said that to depart is to be with Christ (Phil. 1:23). Immediately we are with Jesus. If we are absent from the body, we are at that moment present with the Lord: "We are confident, I say, and willing rather to be absent from the body, and to be present with the Lord" (2 Cor. 5:8).

There with the Savior we wait for the resurrection of our bodies at the return of the glorious King. John sees the souls of the martyrs under the altar: "And when he had opened the fifth seal, I saw under the altar the souls of them that were slain for the word of God, and for the testimony which they held" (Rev. 6:9).

They are not in the fullness of heaven; they are waiting in Paradise. Like Moses in the cleft of the rock, covered by the hand of God, they are safe. The fullness of heaven will be ours when Jesus comes again and our bodies are resurrected. We will be like the Savior, in our immortalized, glorified bodies.

We shall know each other in heaven. It is unthinkable that we should live unknown and unknowing. Intuitive knowledge will introduce us to everybody: "Many shall come from the east and west, and shall sit down with Abraham, and Isaac and Jacob, in the kingdom of heaven" (Matt. 8:11).

How do we know Abraham and Isaac and Jacob? We know them intuitively in the same way that James, John, and Peter knew Moses and Elijah on the Mount of Transfiguration. We shall sit down and visit with the saints and have all eternity in which to enjoy their fellowship. We shall sit down with Adam and talk about Eden. We shall sit down with Noah and talk about the flood. We shall sit down with Moses and talk about the deliverance of the Israelites from the Red Sea. We shall sit down with Elijah and talk about his ride in the chariot of fire. We shall sit down with Lazarus and talk about his resurrection from the dead. We shall sit down with Paul and talk about his life-changing experience on the Damascus Road.

There will be a joyous reunion with our loved ones. The infinitely sad kiss of good-bye at the deathbed and the last longing glance upon the casket will be more than forgotten in the kiss of reunion and welcome at the gate of heaven.

Our treasures to enjoy are there. They are given to us in two ways: by inheritance and by reward. Heaven itself is ours by inheritance. It is not ours by conquest or good works or victorious merit but by the grace and gift of God. Another—namely, our Lord Jesus—has won the heavenly reward for us and given its blessings to us. We once looked from afar—the seed of the serpent, the children of Satan, the offspring of wrath. Then we became the children of God through His grace. We are now heirs by adoption. Our true home is there; our estate is there; our inheritance is there. Through the love of Jesus our Lord, we are fellow heirs and joint heirs with Him: "And if children, then heirs; heirs of God, and joint heirs with Christ; if so be that we suffer with him, that we may be also glorified together" (Rom. 8:17).

And we have treasure in heaven by reward. Our rewards for faithful service are given to us there, not here. We can lay up treasures in heaven:

> Lay not up for yourselves treasures upon earth, where moth and rust doth corrupt, and where thieves break through and steal: But lay up for yourselves treasures in heaven, where neither moth nor rust doth corrupt, and where thieves do not break through nor steal: For where your treasure is, there will your heart be also. (Matt. 6:19-21)

Jesus Will Be There
Not only are the angels of God and the redeemed children

of the Lord in heaven, but also Jesus is there. Heaven is where our Savior is. Where He is, there we shall also be welcomed by Him. With our precious loved ones we shall proceed through the streets of gold through the long lines of loving angels to the throne of our Lord Jesus because He is the One we are eager to see.

> *Oh, Christ, He is the fountain—*
> *The deep, sweet well of love.*
> *The streams of earth I've tasted,*
> *More deep, I'll drink above.*

> *There, in an ocean of fullness,*
> *His mercy doth expand,*
> *And glory, glory dwelleth*
> *In Immanuel's land.*

> *The bride eyes not her garment,*
> *But her dear bridegroom's face.*
> *I will not gaze at glory,*
> *But on my Lord's dear face.*

> *Not at the crown He giveth,*
> *But on His pierced hand;*
> *For the Lamb is all the glory*
> *In Immanuel's land.*

I copied this from the great preacher T. DeWitt Talmadge:

I do not want to go to the skeptics', the rationalists', the materialists' heaven. I would not exchange the poorest room in your house for the finest heaven that Tom Paine, John Mill, Huxley, Darwin, or Ingersoll, those great infidels, ever dreamed of. Their heaven has no Christ in it. All eyes are fixed upon Him. Every look is one of love. Gratitude glows in every bosom. Praise swells in every song. Golden harps resound His worth and merit. The saints cast down their golden crowns at His dear feet saying, "Not unto us but unto Thee be the glory forever and ever."

As the first chapter of the book of Revelation recounts: "Unto him that loved us, and washed us from our sins in his own blood, And hath made us kings and priests unto God and his Father; to him be glory and dominion for ever and ever. Amen" (Rev. 1:5-6).

> After this I beheld, and, lo, a great multitude, which no man could number, of all nations, and kindreds, and people, and tongues, stood before the throne, and before the Lamb, clothed with white robes, and palms in their hands: And cried with a loud voice, saying, Salvation to our God which sitteth upon the throne, and unto the Lamb. And all the angels stood round about the throne, and about the elders and the four beasts, and fell before the throne on their faces, and worshiped God, Saying, Amen: Blessing, and glory, and wisdom, and thanksgiving, and honour, and power, and might be unto our God for ever and ever. Amen. (Rev. 7:9-12)

It will be a blessing for us beyond description to be numbered among that worshipful group.

A little boy was reciting Psalm 23, "The Lord is my shepherd, I shall not want," and he said it like this: "The Lord is my shepherd, He's all that I want." Likewise, Paul said, "Having a desire to depart, and to be with Christ; which is far better" (Phil. 1:23). The author of Hebrews said, "Let us draw near with a true heart in full assurance of faith" (Heb. 10:22). The sainted apostle John said, "Beloved now are we the sons of

God, . . . but we know that, when he shall appear, we shall be like him; for we shall see him as he is" (1 John 3:2).

Let us make ready for the eternity yet to come. In our present lost, carnal, unregenerated nature, we are unfit for heaven. We have been ruined by the fall. By natural birth we are not prepared for heaven. What is a banquet to one who has no appetite? What is a music festival to one who has no hearing? What is the beauty and glory of the firmament to one who is blind? What is the presence of God to one who finds pleasure in fleshly lust? Heaven can be an abhorrent vacuum to the unregenerate. What would the confirmed drunkard do in heaven? What would the glutton do in heaven? What would the whoremonger do in heaven? What would the sensualist do in heaven? What would those who dislike and disdain holy worship services do in heaven when we worship God unceasingly in holy services? The unregenerate desperately need a change of heart, of life, of love, of interest. They need a new nature in Christ. They need to worship and adore the things of God. They need to be saved, to be born again, to be presented to the Lord in glory.

When Lazarus was raised from the grave, he was clothed in grave clothes marked with the signs and the seal of death. And Jesus said, "Loose him, and let him go." We, with our unregenerate, carnal, dying nature, need to cast aside all those robes of decay and death. We need to be clothed with the holy garments of God. Jesus provides these holy garments when we accept Him as Savior.

CHAPTER 3
What I Believe about Heaven: The Pageantry

And he shewed me a pure river of water of life, clear as crystal, proceeding out of the throne of God and of the Lamb. In the midst of the street of it, and on either side of the river, was there the tree of life, which bare twelve manner of fruits, and yielded her fruit every month: and the leaves of the tree were for the healing of the nations. And there shall be no more curse: but the throne of God and of the Lamb shall be in it; and his servants shall serve him: And they shall see his face; and his name shall be in their foreheads. And there shall be no night there; and they need no candle, neither light of the sun; for the Lord God giveth them light: and they shall reign for ever and ever. And he said unto me, These sayings are faithful and true: and the Lord God of the holy prophets sent his angel to shew unto his servants the things which must shortly be done. Behold, I come quickly: blessed is he that keepeth the sayings of the prophecy of this book. (Rev. 22:1-7)

What Shall We Do in Heaven?

The sarcastic unbelievers answer, "Nothing." This insulting travesty is often depicted and pictured as contemptuous satire. There is not any one of us who has not seen again and again a cartoon about a man with wings and a halo around his head seated on a fleecy cloud, strumming a harp. Could such a grotesque parody and ridiculous burlesque be true of heaven? Could it be a place where we resign ourselves to endless ages of nothingness and the boredom which would naturally follow? Are we forced to look forward to nothingness? Does a Christian nirvana of inevitable nothingness await us? Are we graduated into a paradise of inactive nothingness? Is heaven nothing more than a scrap heap of worn-out bodies or a collection of human entities consigned to the endless boredom of nothingness? "Blessed are the dead which die in the Lord from henceforth: Yea, saith the Spirit, that they may rest from their labours; and their works do follow them" (Rev. 14:13).

Does rest mean nothingness? No! By "rest" we mean deliverance from sin, temptation, weakness, failure, and defeat. We shall rest in God's grace and love and in the joy of our heavenly assignments. The very word *rest* implies the word *labor*, which is in the verse above ("They may rest from their labours"). We shall work without weariness; we shall still be refreshed after the toil of the day and of the century and even of the forever.

Jesus Answers Our Questions

Service and unfailing rewards are basic themes in Christ's teaching.

Who then is a faithful and wise servant, whom his
lord hath made ruler over his household, to give them
meat in due season? Blessed is that servant, whom
his lord when he cometh [he is talking about the end
of the age] shall find so doing. Verily I say unto you,
That he shall make him ruler over all his goods. (Matt.
24:45-47)

Consider the next chapter.

> And so he that had received five talents came and said,
> Lord, thou deliveredst unto me two talents: behold, I
> have gained two other talents beside them. His lord said
> unto him, Well done, good and faithful servant; thou
> has been faithful over a few things, I will make thee
> ruler over many things: enter thou into the joy of thy
> lord. (Matt. 25:20-23)

A similar message is found in Luke.

> And it came to pass, that when he was returned, having
> received the kingdom, then he commanded these servants
> to be called unto him, to whom he had given the money,
> that he might know how much every man had gained
> by trading.Then came the first, saying, Lord, thy pound
> hath gained ten pounds. And he said unto him, Well,
> thou good servant: because thou hast been faithful in a
> very little, have thou authority over ten cities [in the
> world to come]. And the second came, saying, Lord,
> thy pound hath gained five pounds. And he said likewise
> to him, Be thou also over five cities. (Luke 19:15-19)

Therefore, assignments will be made in glory according to a
man's ability to reign and to rule.

Jesus is the great instructor. He teaches us to use the money
and means of this life for service and advancement in the life to
come.

> And I say unto you, Make to yourselves friends of the
> mammon of unrighteousness; that, when ye fail [when
> the riches fail and you come to the end of life], they
> may receive you into everlasting habitations. (Luke 16:9)

That means that when in death riches are gone, those you have blessed and benefited by your ministries here in this world will welcome you in heaven. The work here is to prepare for our greater rewards over there.

We have a picture of our work assignments in the heavenly world in the life and work of Jesus Himself. Hebrews 13:8 is one of the great verses in the Bible: "Jesus Christ the same yesterday, and today, and for ever."

Jesus Christ is the same *yesterday*. In His preexistent state He worked; He created the heavens and the earth—every firmament, every star, every planet. The Son of God did this creative activity as the preincarnate Christ.

Jesus Christ is the same *today*. In His earthly life He was a workman, a carpenter. In His ministry He toiled day and night. Today in heaven He is the great intercessor, the head of the church, the Savior of the body.

Jesus Christ is the same *forever*. He will be King and Lord over a vast re-created universe—a heaven and an earth filled with teeming, laboring, serving, reigning people.

The model work-ministry of our Lord finds repercussion in the heavenly assignments of His redeemed people: "But Jesus answered them, My Father worketh hitherto, and I work" (John 5:17). "Verily, verily, I say unto you, He that believeth on me, the works that I do shall he do also; and greater works than these shall he do; because I go unto my Father" (John 14:12).

Well, what are these heavenly works and glorious assignments we shall have in the other world? He says we shall be judges in the re-created world with Christ.

> And Jesus said unto them, Verily I say unto you, That ye which have followed me, in the regeneration [the re-creation of this heaven and earth] when the Son of man shall sit in the throne of his glory, ye also shall sit upon twelve thrones, judging the twelve tribes of Israel. (Matt. 19:28)

Do ye not know that the saints shall judge the world? and if the world shall be judged by you, are ye unworthy to judge the smallest matters? Know ye not that we shall judge angels? how much more things that pertain to this life? (1 Cor. 6:2-3)

That vast, innumerable, multitudinous throng of angels are to be judged by us. We shall reign and rule with Christ throughout the endless succession of ages: "It is a faithful saying: For if we be dead with him, we shall also live with him: If we suffer, we shall also reign with him" (2 Tim. 2:11-12). "And has made us unto our God kings and priests: and we shall reign on the earth" (Rev. 5:10).

We shall reign in this created heaven above and over this renewed earth on which we plant our feet.

According to Luke 19, some of us will rule over ten cities, and some of us over five cities, but each of us shall have our respective assignment: "And there shall be no more curse: but the throne of God and of the Lamb shall be in it; and his servants shall serve him" (Rev. 22:3).

We shall have a place of honor next to the King such as the servants described in Esther 1:14: they "saw the king's face and . . . sat first in the kingdom."

We shall not be passive spectators, just observing; but we shall be an active, vital part of the whole re-created kingdom of God. We each shall have a service to render according to how God has made us and endowed us. As we differ in tastes, likes, looks, choices, and abilities, so also we shall differ in our separate assignments and activities.

The Bible Reveals the Continuity of Life
Let us consider the biblical revelation of the continuity of life. When the shadow of this life is over, the real life begins

there, in the land beyond. There is progress in the pursuit of the purpose of God for us in the rich meaning of life on a higher level. What we have begun on earth, we shall consummate in heaven.

We shall be the same persons there as here; otherwise, a heavenly life has no meaning. I will be I; you will be you; we shall be we. If that is not so, it has no meaning at all. Our traits, abilities, and personalities will be the same; only they will be redeemed and glorified.

The poignant example of this is seen in the resurrected, glorified life of our Lord Jesus. He was the same Lord Jesus in His resurrected life as He was in the days of His flesh. His recognitions were human. As He was when He walked in our midst, so He was when He was glorified and raised from the dead. For example, He said in Luke: "Behold my hands and my feet, that it is I myself: handle me, and see; for a spirit hath not flesh and bones, as ye see me have" (Luke 24:39).

He was the same Lord Jesus; He was human. He was recognized by John because of the way He folded a napkin. When John saw that napkin folded in a certain way, he knew that Jesus was raised from the dead. Jesus was recognized by Mary because of the way He pronounced her name. He was recognized by the two disciples in Emmaus because of the way He said a blessing. Nobody said a blessing just like the Lord Jesus. His hand was recognized by the disciples on the Sea of Galilee because of the miraculous draft of fish they caught. He was the same human being—the Lord Jesus. Accordingly, we shall be the same persons with our respective faculties, abilities, and personalities. We shall continue developing and progressing in the world to come.

Mozart died at thirty-five years of age. Are the gifts he possessed in this life to vanish away in the life to come? Is his genius to be separated from the man himself? The great musician will still be Mozart in the life beyond.

Raphael died at thirty-seven years of age. But, he will still be recognized as Raphael in the afterlife. Is his sublime career to be obliterated and forgotten? The great painter will still be Raphael.

Samuel Stennett, a Baptist pastor in London, died in the prime of his ministry. He wrote many beautiful hymns, including "On Jordan's Stormy Banks I Stand" and "Majestic Sweetness Sits Enthroned." In heaven, will he cast his gift of song away? The book of the Revelation constantly speaks of "the new songs" that we shall sing.

> And they sung a new song, saying, Thou art worthy
> to take the book, and to open the seals thereof: for
> thou wast slain, and hast redeemed us to God by
> thy blood out of every kindred, and tongue, and
> people, and nation. (Rev. 5:9)

> And they sung as it were a new song before the throne,
> and before the four beasts, and the elders: and no
> man could learn that song but the hundred and forty
> and four thousand, which were redeemed from the
> earth. (Rev. 14:3)

> And they sing the song of Moses the servant of
> God, and the song of the Lamb, saying, Great and
> marvellous are thy works, Lord God Almighty; just
> and true are thy ways, thou King of saints. (Rev.
> 15:3)

The Revelation contains more songs than any other book of the Bible except the hymn book of Psalms, and even in the Psalms the "new songs" are constantly referenced:

> Sing unto him a new song; play skilfully with a loud
> noise. (Ps. 33:3)

And he hath put a new song in my mouth, even praise unto our God: many shall see it, and fear, and shall trust in the Lord. (Ps. 40:3)

I will praise the name of God with a song, and will magnify him with thanksgiving. (Ps. 69:30)

O sing unto the Lord a new song: sing unto the Lord, all the earth." (Ps. 96:1)

O sing unto the Lord a new song; for he hath done marvellous things: his right hand, and his holy arm, hath gotten him the victory. (Ps. 98:1)

I will sing a new song unto thee, O God: upon a psaltery and an instrument of ten strings will I sing praises unto thee. (Ps. 144:9)

Praise ye the Lord. Sing unto the Lord a new song, and his praise in the congregation of saints. (Ps. 149:1)

We shall keep on writing and singing "the new songs," and it will be an avenue of praising our Lord God throughout all of the eternal ages.

Our lives, talents, gifts, and abilities shall continue to be developed throughout all the ages. In heaven we shall be permitted to finish tasks we had dreamed to do but have had no opportunity or time or strength or ability to finish on earth.

The great astronomer O. M. Mitchell believed that in the future life he would go from world to world and planet to planet continuing his study of astronomy. What a glorious assignment—to study the Lord's infinite creation forever, to sit at the feet of the Creator himself and learn what God has done! Like him, we shall also ascend out of the narrow, circumscribed valley of life into the infinitely broader expanse of the glory of God above us, beyond us, and around us.

Life and work here on earth is interrupted by death. We get old and we die right in the midst of our assignments. As Cecil Rhodes said in his last words before he died, "So little done, so much to do; we shall continue in heaven."

The injustices and inequalities of this life plead for another recompensing creation. A good God could not leave us a prey to a leering devil in a ruined universe. The moral law, found not only in God but also deeply rooted in us, demands a vindication of adjustment after death.

There are people in this life with talents never seen or used. Many have a cherished gift but take no opportunity to use it. They are like a winged bird placed in a cage. There are poets, philosophers, and singers whose talents and gifts were lost in a coffin and buried in a grave. But they will get their chance to come into their own in heaven. God did not create and endow us here in order to cast us away there. The great abounding triumphant life is beyond death.

We sing this glorious song:

> *There is no disappointment in heaven*
> *No weariness, sorrow or pain;*
> *No hearts that are bleeding and broken,*
> *No song with a minor refrain.*
> *The clouds of our earthly horizon*
> *Will never appear in the sky,*
> *For all will be sunshine and gladness*
> *With never a sob nor a sigh.*
>
> *There will never be crepe on the door knob,*
> *No funeral trains in the sky.*
> *No graves on the hillsides of glory,*
> *For there we shall never more die.*
> *The old will be young there forever,*
> *Transformed in a moment of time.*

Immortal we'll stand in His likeness,
The stars and the sun to outshine.

I'm bound for that beautiful city
My Lord has prepared for His own.
Where all the redeemed of all ages
Sing "Glory" around the white throne.
Sometimes I grow homesick for heaven,
And the glories I there shall behold.
What a joy that will be when my Savior I see
In that beautiful city of gold.

The consummation is in glory—there, not here. We will never know or experience ultimate glory in this life and in this world.

A Summary

There are two possessions we shall carry into the forever, beyond the grave: (1) our character, since we are redeemed by the blood of the Crucified One, and (2) our capacity, since we are endowed by the Lord God Himself. Shall these gifts from the creative hand of God be wantonly wasted, discarded in uselessness and forgetfulness? Shall we be consigned to a forever of idleness and nothingness? No, a thousand times no!

Alfred Lord Tennyson wrote a poem in the last days of his life and asked that this poem be printed at the conclusion of each of his published works:

Sunset and evening star,
And one clear call to me!
And may there be no moaning
  of the bar,
When I put out to sea,

But such a tide as moving seems asleep,
Too full for sound and foam,
When that which drew from out the boundless deep
Turns again home.

Twilight and evening bell,
And after that the dark!
And may there be no sadness of farewell,
When I embark;

For though from out our bourne of time
    and place
The flood may bear me far,
I hope to see my Pilot face to face
When I have crossed the bar.

Death does not end in defeat and tragedy for us, but all believers shall experience triumph and victory at the conclusion of their lives.

Just before 1890, at the end of Robert Browning's life, he also wrote a poem and asked that this "Epilogue" conclude all his published works:

One who never turned his back but marched
    breast forward,
Never doubted clouds would break,
Never dreamed, though right were worsted,
    wrong would triumph,
Held we fall to rise, are baffled to fight better,
Sleep to wake.

No, at noonday in the bustle of man's work-time,
Greet the unseen with a cheer!
Bid him forward, breast and back as either
    should be,

"Strive and thrive!" Cry, "Speed,—fight on,
  fare ever
There as here!"

What a gloriously good thing God hath prepared as He purposed for us an upper and better world. Our lives, though broken by death here, continue unbroken up there.

CHAPTER 4
What I Believe about Heaven:
Its Inexpressible Preciousness

For to me to live is Christ, and to die is gain. But if I live in the flesh, this is the fruit of my labour: yet what I shall choose I wot not. For I am in a strait betwixt two, having a desire to depart, and to be with Christ; which is far better. (Phil. 1:21-23)

These are the words Paul wrote in Philippians. Then these are the last words Paul wrote to Timothy, his son in the ministry:

> For I am now ready to be offered, and the time of my departure is at hand. I have fought a good fight, I have finished my course, I have kept the faith: Henceforth there is laid up for me a crown of righteousness, which the Lord, the righteous judge, shall give me at that day: and not to me only, but unto all them also that love his appearing. (2 Tim. 4:6-8)

Many questions are asked about heaven. The answers to these questions have to be found in the Bible. There is no other infallible source of revelation.

Will We Know Each Other in Heaven?
A baby is born into a home. The grandmother dies; she

is expecting that baby to follow her to heaven. Several years later an older brother dies; he is expecting a little child to join him in heaven. The years pass and the mother dies; she is expecting a reunion with the teenager she left behind. After the years pass and the baby has grown to manhood, he marries, and his wife dies; she is expecting to see her husband in heaven. Other years pass and a grandchild dies; that child is expecting to meet his grandfather in heaven. This is the same person—a baby, a child, a teenager, a husband, a grandfather.

We will know each other in heaven by intuitive knowledge, which is a gift of God. Moses and Elijah appeared on the Mount of Transfiguration (Luke 9:31). How did Peter, James, and John know them? These saints had been dead for a thousand years. They knew them by intuitive knowledge. God gave them a worthy introduction to these Old Testament saints: "And I say unto you, That many shall come from the east and west, and shall sit down with Abraham, and Isaac, and Jacob, in the kingdom of heaven" (Matt. 8:11).

Abraham and Isaac and Jacob will be recognized through intuitive knowledge: "For now we see through a glass darkly; but then face to face: now I know in part; but then shall I know even as also I am known" (1 Cor. 13:12).

We shall not know less of each other in heaven; we shall know more. In fact, we shall not really know the full circumference and parameters of life until we get to heaven. "He that overcometh, the same shall be clothed in white raiment; and I will not blot out his name out of the book of life, but I will confess his name before my Father, and before his angels" (Rev. 3:5).

We shall possess our individual names in heaven. We shall be known as individuals. You will be you; I shall be I; we shall be we. Personality and individuality exist beyond the grave.

Do Those in Heaven Know
What Is Happening on Earth?

In heaven we shall have a knowledge of what is developing on earth.

> Wherefore seeing we also are compassed about with so
> great a cloud of witnesses, let us lay aside every weight,
> and the sin which doth so easily beset us, and let us run
> with patience the race that is set before us. (Heb. 12:1)

This passage certainly does not deny that the saints in heaven look down upon us in our earthly pilgrimage. Samuel was in the other world (heaven); yet he knew what was developing between King Saul and Israel in the earthly domain (1 Sam. 28:16-18).

> I say unto you, that likewise joy shall be in heaven over
> one sinner that repenteth, more than over ninety and
> nine just persons, which need no repentance. Likewise,
> I say unto you, there is joy in the presence of the angels
> of God over one sinner that repenteth. (Luke 15:7, 10)

Who are these rejoicing in the presence of the angels of God? They are the redeemed saints in glory. When someone gives his heart to Jesus, those in heaven see that response of faith and commitment and rejoice in unspeakable gladness over that one who has found life in the Lord.

> And it came to pass, that the beggar died, and was car-
> ried by the angels into Abraham's bosom: the rich man
> also died, and was buried; And in hell he lift up his eyes,
> being in torments, and seeth Abraham afar off, and
> Lazarus in his bosom. Then he said, I pray thee there-
> fore, father, that thou wouldest send him to my father's

house; For I have five brethren; that he may testify unto them, lest they also come into this place of torment. (Luke 16:22-23, 27-28)

Even while in Hades, the rich man knows that his five brothers are still lost.

And when he had opened the fifth seal, I saw under the altar the souls of them that were slain for the word of God, and for the testimony which they held: And they cried with a loud voice, saying, How long, O Lord, holy and true, dost thou not judge and avenge our blood on them that dwell on the earth? (Rev. 6:9-10)

Those in heaven know what is happening on this earth, and they follow those events with the most intense interest.

Will We Know if Our Loved Ones Do Not Arrive in Heaven?

How can we be happy if someone dear to us in this life dies without Christ? These unsaved loved ones will not be remembered. It will be as if they never lived. There is no life or existence outside Christ.

Thou shalt blot out the remembrance of Amalek from under heaven. (Deut. 25:19)

Thou hast rebuked the heathen, thou hast destroyed the wicked, thou hast put out their name for ever and ever. (Ps. 9:5)

Let them be blotted out of the book of the living, and not be written with the righteous. (Ps. 69:28)

Let his posterity be cut off; and in the generation following let their name be blotted out. (Ps. 109:13)

This is the tragedy of family members who are not Christians.

Will Our Marriages Remain Intact in Heaven?

If a man had two wives on earth or if a woman had two
husbands on earth, in heaven will he have both wives and will she
have both husbands? This question was asked of the Lord Jesus
by the Sadducees in their scorn for the doctrine of the resurrection
of the dead. They referred to the law of the Levirate marriage
whereby the closest male relation of a man who died was required
to marry his brother's widow and raise up children to the deceased
(see Matt. 22:23-30). In this instance, which was presented
sarcastically by the Sadducees, the widow had seven different
brothers as her husband respectively. When one brother died
without a child, the other brother had to take her as his wife. When
he died without an offspring, the next brother had to marry her.
The Sadducees concluded their illustration with this question:
"Therefore in the resurrection whose wife shall she be of the
seven? for they all had her" (Matt. 22:28).

Full of scorn, derision, and disdain for the Lord who was
preaching the resurrection of the dead, they must have been
laughing as they baited Jesus with a loaded question, based
upon the assumption that earthly marriage would be perpetuated in heaven. Jesus answered by dismissing the perpetuation
of husband-wife relationships in heaven: "For in the resurrection they neither marry, nor are given in marriage, but are as
the angels of God in heaven" (Matt. 22:30).

Angels are persons but not sexual beings. They do not
procreate. They do not share sexual intimacy, nor shall we in
heaven. Marriage as a physical union is terminated with the
death of one spouse (see Rom. 7:1-3; 1 Cor. 7:39). Sexual

intimacy is not necessary for one's knowledge and enjoyment of another. I loved and knew my mother with no thought of sexual intimacy. Such would have been unthinkable and unimaginable. I loved and knew my father with no thought of sexual intimacy. I loved and knew my brothers and sisters with no thought of sexual intimacy. I love and know the members of my congregation deeply and preciously so, with no thought of sexual intimacy. I love and know the Lord Jesus with no thought of sexual intimacy. Surely in heaven the relationship between the glorified believer and Christ will supersede and overshadow every earthly fellowship and pleasure previously shared. Our focus will move from earthly spouse and physical intimacy to heavenly king and spiritual communion.

Consider what Sarah said when the angel came to her and to Abraham in their old age, saying that they would have a child: "Therefore Sarah laughed within herself, saying, After I am waxed old shall I have pleasure [as they did when they were first married], my lord being old also?" (Gen. 18:12)

Abraham was ninety-nine years old, and Sarah was eighty-nine years old. Though sexual intimacy seemingly was no longer a priority between the two, they still loved each other and were blessed by each other. In heaven, though husband and wife are no longer sexually intimate, they shall know and enjoy and appreciate each other in the life of the Lord.

Will Jesus Be the Only Person of the Trinity We Shall See in Heaven?

Yes. There is one God and only one. We shall not see three Gods in heaven. In Deuteronomy, we read the famous *Shema* of Israel: "Hear, O Israel: The Lord our God is one Lord" (Deut. 6:4). The only God we shall ever feel in our hearts is the Holy Spirit. We are told to "be filled with the Spirit" (Eph. 5:18) as we experience Christ's living in us:

But ye are not in the flesh, but in the Spirit, if so be that the Spirit of God dwell in you. Now if any man have not the Spirit of Christ, he is none of his. And if Christ be in you, the body is dead because of sin; but the Spirit is life because of righteousness. (Rom. 8:9-10)

And ye became followers of us, and of the Lord, having received the word in much affliction, with joy of the Holy Ghost. (1 Thess. 1:6)

The gladness, the exaltation, the unspeakable ecstasy of God's filling your heart comes through the Holy Spirit. The only God we shall ever see is the Lord Jesus. When you look at him, you see God: "He that hath seen me hath seen the Father; and how sayest thou then, Show us the Father?" (John 14:9).

Will Our Savior Have Nail-Scarred Hands in Heaven?

Yes, the scars from the nails that pierced the hands of the Savior are there for us to see:

Behold my hands and my feet, that it is I myself: handle me, and see; for a spirit hath not flesh and bones, as ye see me have. And when he had thus spoken, he shewed them his hands and his feet (Luke 24:39-40).

The other disciples therefore said unto him [Thomas], We have seen the Lord. But he said unto them, Except I shall see in his hands the print of the nails, and put my finger into the print of the nails, and thrust my hand into his side, I will not believe. Then saith he [Jesus] to Thomas, Reach hither thy finger, and behold my hands; and reach hither thy hand, and thrust it into my side; and be not faithless, but believing. And Thomas answered and said unto him, My Lord and my God. (John 20:25, 27-28)

Just as the little distinctive personalities and forms and figures and configurations make you unique, so it is with the Lord.

There was a time when the risen Lord Jesus was not recognized. Speaking of the two disciples in Emmaus, Luke says: "But their eyes were holden that they should not know him" (Luke 24:16). John, speaking of Mary Magdalene, writes:

> And they [the two angels] say unto her, Woman, why weepest thou? She saith unto them, Because they have taken away my Lord, and I know not where they have laid him. And when she had thus said, she turned herself back, and saw Jesus standing, and knew not that it was Jesus. (John 20:13-14)

> But when the morning was now come, Jesus stood on the shore: but the disciples knew not that it was Jesus. (John 21:4)

But all of this was for an earthly moment. Jesus revealed Himself to those whom He loved and to those who loved Him in His chosen time and way.

 Can You Eat All You Want in Heaven and Not Get Fat?

The answer is a glorious amen and yes! I hope we are going to eat in heaven all the time. In heaven as I walk those golden streets, I'm going to have a sign hanging around my neck reading, "Feed the pastor!" As a young preacher, I made more friends around the family dinner table than by any other activity of my ministry. I never turned down an invitation to a meal. If a family invited me, I was there at the table.

> And while they yet believed not for joy, and wondered, he said unto them, Have ye here any meat? And they

gave him a piece of a broiled fish, and of a honeycomb. And he took it, and did eat before them. (Luke 24:41-43)

And he saith unto me, Write, Blessed are they which are called unto the marriage supper of the Lamb. (Rev. 19:9)

In the midst of the street of it, and on either side of the river, was there the tree of life, which bare twelve manner of fruits, and yielded her fruit every month: and the leaves of the tree were for the healing of the nations. (Rev. 22:2)

This brings to mind the miracle of assimilation or constructive metabolism. You are what you eat. If you do not believe that, observe what happens to you if you quit eating for a while. You are a monument to bread and beans and garlic and pepper and all the other things you consume. Dead, inanimate matter, by a miracle of assimilation or metabolism, is quickened into you.

The food we eat in our resurrected, glorified bodies is raised and quickened one step and level higher. It becomes a miraculous part of the glorified body. This miracle of eating inanimate food so that it becomes me, full of thought and emotion and will, is no greater than the miracle of the translation of the heavenly food we ingest into our glorified bodies. God performs this miracle in which our glorified bodies are adaptive to but not dependent upon consumption of food. However, the focus of heaven will not be on food and eating but rather on Jesus, "the Bread of Life." Though eating food is possible, feeding on the Word of God will satisfy our appetites in a more exciting way.

Will Angels Escort Us to Heaven?

"And it came to pass, that the beggar died, and was carried by the angels into Abraham's bosom" (Luke 16:22).

When a believer dies an angel will escort him to heaven. Though one might lose his way, that angel will guide and escort him, opening to him the gate of heaven.

Will We Go to Heaven or to an Intermediate State When We Die?

At the time of death one goes to an intermediate state called "paradise" to await the resurrection of the body. Paul uses the words *paradise* and *heaven* interchangeably.

> I knew a man in Christ above fourteen years ago,
> (whether in the body, I cannot tell; or whether out of
> the body, I cannot tell: God knoweth:) such an one
> caught up to the third heaven. How that he was caught
> up into paradise, and heard unspeakable words, which
> it is not lawful for a man to utter. (2 Cor. 12:2, 4)

Where Jesus is will be heaven enough; and when we die, we go to paradise where we wait with Jesus for the resurrection of our glorified bodies, which will be given to us when Jesus comes with His saints. That will be heaven for us.

Do People Who Commit Suicide Go to Heaven?

Samuel says to Saul, who on that day committed suicide:

> Moreover the Lord will also deliver Israel with thee into
> the hand of the Philistines: and tomorrow shalt thou and
> thy sons be with me: the Lord also shall deliver the host
> of Israel into the hand of the Philistines. (1 Sam. 28:19)

One can be sick in any part of his living existence—in the head, foot, heart, hand, or torso. But he can also be sick in the mind and soul. Anyone who commits suicide is desperately ill.

Does God hate one who is sick? Does He disown one because he is not well?

Jesus is the Great Physician. He will complete healing in body and in soul in heaven. The retarded will be retarded no more. The crippled will be crippled no longer. The sick in mind will be tortured no more. The one who has accepted Jesus Christ as personal Savior will be in heaven, even if he dies by his own hand.

Do Homosexuals Go to Heaven?

Heaven is a holy place adorned by the presence of our Savior himself. Though immorality may be observed, tolerated, and even embraced on earth, in heaven it will not be practiced; it will be intolerable; it will be totally banned (See Heb. 12:14; Rev. 21:8; 22:15).

We are all tempted to sin; we must all ask God for strength to overcome sin and to remain chaste and pure. According to Romans 1:26-28, homosexuality is the most aberrant form of sin, but anyone who repents of sin, however aberrant it may be, can experience the new birth and go to heaven, not as a homosexual but as a redeemed sinner. Jesus is ready to save anyone who calls upon Him in repentance and faith.

Will Animals Go to Heaven?

The Bible says that the Garden of Eden, called paradise, was filled with animals:

> And God made the beast of the earth after his kind, and cattle after their kind, and every thing that creepeth upon the earth after his kind: and God saw that it was good. (Gen. 1:25)

> And out of the ground the Lord God formed every beast of the field, and every fowl of the air; and brought

them unto Adam to see what he would call them: and whatsoever Adam called every living creature, that was the name thereof. (Gen. 2:19)

Animals have been an integral part of earthly life, testifying to the creative genius of the Lord Himself. The millennium is described as being at peace with the whole animal world.

> The wolf also shall dwell with the lamb, and the leopard shall lie down with the kid; and the calf and the young lion and the fatling together; and a little child shall lead them. And the cow and the bear shall feed; their young ones shall lie down together; and the lion shall eat straw like the ox. And the sucking child shall play on the hole of the asp, and the weaned child shall put his hand on the cockatrice den. They shall not hurt nor destroy in all my holy mountain: for the earth shall be full of the knowledge of the Lord, as the waters cover the sea. (Isa. 11:6-9)

Romans 8:19-23 speaks of the deliverance of the whole creation. The burned-out planets, the barren deserts, and the fallen humanity—all of God's creation will be delivered. The whole creation of God, including pets, animals, and the entire creation of the living God, will be delivered from corruption. Heaven will be a beautiful Edenic paradise for us all, for every living thing.

Since we are not aware of any animal's resurrection from the dead, we have no evidence that specific pets of yesteryear will be in heaven. The idea that attachment to family pets would be so strong that one could not think of heaven without the beloved dog or cat originates in the ancient pagan civilizations, who even prepared replicas of their domestic pets to place in their tombs for the afterlife. Nevertheless, as we look to our heavenly abode, our focus must be on fellowship with Jesus above all else. He forever will be the main attraction of heaven. Of course, God has shown a penchant for varieties of life forms, and it would be difficult to imagine that this would not be perpetuated in the heavenlies. Still, however, in heaven our focus moves from creation to redemption, and the redeemed made in His image and committed to Him in faith will lead the praise and testimony.

What Is the New Heaven and the New Earth (Rev. 21:1)?

Matter is everlasting and indestructible. The creation will be re-created in perfection, just as our bodies, which can decay or be burned, will be remade and resurrected.

Jesus spoke of this re-creation as "regeneration" (Matt. 19:28). Peter spoke of it as "restitution" (Acts 3:21). Peter wrote of it as "reserved unto fire" (2 Pet. 3:6-7, 10). This earth as you see it and this universe as you look upon it will be re-created as God reconstructed it in the beginning.

The "New Jerusalem," our eternal and heavenly home, will come down from God out of heaven. From our mansion in this city, along with Jesus, we shall rule the universe with its teeming multitudes of angels and saints and cities.

The resurrected Jesus in an instant could be anywhere. So we shall be able in an instant to be anywhere in the re-created universe. The whole creation of God will be ours over which to rule and reign. We, as the angels, shall keep on learning throughout eternity (1 Pet. 1:12). We shall keep on serving along with our fellow saints, using our different talents and abilities (Matt. 25:15; Rev. 22:3). We shall work and labor and toil for God without tears, sadness, regret, weariness, or failure. Failure, regret, defeat, disappointment, and weariness belong to the veil of tears on this earth, but they do not belong to heaven (Rev. 14:13; 21:4).

Why Do I Fear Death and Going to Heaven?

This is God's way of keeping us at our assigned tasks in this present world and work. Intuitively we draw back from death, which is a frightful enemy, the last one to be destroyed (1 Cor. 15:26). God never created us to die. Death is an intruder; it is an interloper; it is a curse. God calls it an enemy. We shrink from death because it is abhorrent to us.

Our shortcomings, weaknesses, and sins make us hesitate before facing the Great Judge of all the earth. Although we are Christians, saved by the blood of the Crucified One, we all are sinners. God says that our sins are completely blotted out and remembered against us no more, and we do not need to fear when the day comes for us to stand before Him.

> I, even I, am he that blotteth out thy transgressions for mine own sake, and will not remember thy sins. (Isa. 43:25)

> I have blotted out, as a thick cloud, thy transgressions, and, as a cloud, thy sins: return unto me; for I have redeemed thee. (Isa. 44:22)

Jesus said: "For this is my blood of the new testament, which is shed for many for the remission of sins" (Matt. 26:28).

Paul wrote: "But God commendeth his love toward us, in that, while we were yet sinners, Christ died for us. For if, when were enemies, we were reconciled to God by the death of his Son, much more, being reconciled, we shall be saved by his life" (Rom 5:8, 10). No wonder we sing this marvelous hymn:

Glory, I'm saved;
Glory, I'm saved.
My sins are all pardoned
My guilt is all gone.

Glory, I'm saved;
Glory, I'm saved.
Saved by blood of the Crucified One.

There is life for a look at the Crucified One,
There is life at this moment for thee.
Then look, sinner, look unto Him and be saved,
Unto Him who was nailed to the tree.

What a marvelous thing God has done for us, and what an incomparable and inexpressible prospect God holds before us in His goodness and in His grace!

CHAPTER 5

My Personal Thoughts about Heaven: An Interview with W. A. Criswell, by Dorothy Patterson

Patterson: Kenneth Woodward, in a recent *Newsweek* article on "Heaven," said that preachers today say little about heaven because they are hesitant to describe places that neither they nor anyone has actually seen. Theologian Douglas Stuart from Gordon-Conwell Seminary suggested that another reason for the lack of information on heaven stems from the fact that many clergymen simply don't believe in an afterlife themselves.

On the other hand, public opinion polls have confirmed that, despite agnostics in the pulpit, there are believers in pews. Most Americans not only believe in God but also anticipate some kind of heaven. In a recent *Newsweek* poll, 94 percent believe in God, 77 percent believe in heaven, and 75 percent rated their chances of getting to heaven as good or excellent.

Pastor, do you remember your first awareness of the place called heaven?

Criswell: I grew up in a godly home, and I never missed any service at the church. The sermons that the pastor and visiting evangelists preached often called attention to heaven. In those days, a child's death was not uncommon. I can so well remember going to the funeral for one of my little playmates. The death of my playmate was overwhelming, and the preacher's assurance that this little child was in heaven was puzzling. I had no cause to disbelieve what the preacher said because I had been taught to believe that he preached the pure, unadulterated gospel. Nevertheless, I had no real understanding of the heavenly abode.

Patterson: **What is your concept of heavenly rewards?**

Criswell: When a Christian dies, the judgment that he faces is not a judgment in the sense of whether he or she is going to be saved or lost. When the Christian faces the *bema* (Greek), literally "judgment seat," of the Lord God, it is a place for rewards (2 Cor. 5:10; Rom. 14:10; cf. 1 Cor. 3:13).

We are all judged as to whether we are lost or saved in this world—not up there, not finally by and by, but in the present here and now. When the Christian stands before the *bema* of God, he is given his rewards according to his faithfulness of work and service to God here in this life.

The lost man is judged according to the depths of the punishment that he will endure at the Great White Throne Judgment (Matt. 25:32-46). The man who continually does evil is going to suffer far more than the man who is just lost. The rewards that we are given in heaven or in torment are very real, and they differ a great deal according to the life that we have lived here.

Patterson: **Is heaven an inheritance?**

Criswell: Heaven is the inheritance Jesus has bequeathed to us, in His loving grace and mercy, through His suffering and death. We are going to inherit the whole creation of the Lord, re-created and redeemed. In the heavenly city, we will have a home—a mansion (John 14:1-3).

Patterson: I remember hearing about the little city girl who was visiting the country for the first time. Looking at the night sky she exclaimed, "Oh, Mother, if heaven is so beautiful on the wrong side, what must it be like on the right side!" **Where is heaven located? How do you picture its physical appearance?**

Criswell: All we know about the location of heaven is that Jesus is there. According to the book of Acts, He went *up* to heaven (Acts 1:9). The universe is so infinitely large that beyond the starry spheres we are able to locate an infinitude of continuation out and beyond. God is building a beautiful city, which will come down to this earth out of the great infinitude above.

Patterson: The word *heaven* is found more frequently in the book of Revelation than any other New Testament book. **Is there a description of how heaven will look?**

Criswell: There is indeed an incomparably beautiful presentation in the book of Revelation, chapters 21–22, in which John meticulously describes the New Jerusalem, the City of God, which will be our home.

Patterson: **Do you think the streets are really going to be made out of pure gold?**

Criswell: Well, that is what the Book says, and since I don't know any different, I will accept the Word of God.

Heaven is going to be beautiful and glorious. John first described its parameters: fifteen hundred miles high, fifteen hundred miles wide and fifteen hundred miles in length. I believe this city is uniquely tiered with one vast level and then another. Its inherent light, of course, is the presence of God.

Patterson: **Would Paul's description of that third heaven be a third floor?**

Criswell: Yes, I believe those fifteen hundred miles of its height include one level or story after another. It will be infinitely capable of holding the vast population who will receive the heavenly inheritance.

Patterson: **After the Lord returns, will heaven be strictly above us, or is there going to be a part of heaven here on the earth? Is this earth going to be a part of that many-storied heaven?**

Criswell: The earth is certainly going to be a part of the re-creation of God. It will be a new earth and a new heaven. All the creation of God that has fallen is going to be redeemed and remade, re-created as it was in the beginning. But the City of God is coming down and will hang above the earth.

Patterson: Lewis Sperry Chafer once commented that anyone can devise a plan by which good people may go to heaven; whereas only God can devise a plan by which a sinner, who is his enemy, can go to heaven. Those who have separated themselves from him in the past, can come to him, be redeemed, and go to heaven. Heaven is a place prepared for those who are prepared for it. **Who resides in heaven now, and who do you think is going to live there throughout eternity?**

Criswell: In my humble persuasion, as I read the Word of God, heaven is being constructed now by our Lord Jesus and whomever He invites to work with Him. However, no one is in the heaven of heavens now. When a believer dies he goes to *sheol* or *hades*. *Hades* is divided into two parts—paradise, or Abraham's bosom, and the place of torment. The heaven of heavens will not be ours until the end of the age.

Patterson: **Will there be cherubim and seraphim with us there?**

Criswell: The Bible says that there will be myriads of myriads, tens of thousands times tens of thousands in the heavenly host—so many angels that you cannot count them.

Patterson: **Are there going to be any animals in heaven— Jonah's whale, Abraham's ram, Noah's dove, not to mention all our household pets.**

Criswell: Well, I am a literalist, and when I read the Bible, unless it expressly explains that this is symbolic, I take it for what it claims to be, a literal presentation. When you read Isaiah 11, you surely get the idea that there are going to be animals in glory. When God made the first paradise in the Garden of Eden, He created the animals first and afterward created the man. For us to think of heaven as being a place filled with beautiful animals—the lion and the leopard, for example—is a precious and natural prospect.

Patterson: **Will we know our loved ones who have gone on before—parents, spouses, children? Will we enjoy their companionship in heaven?**

Criswell: Without a doubt, this is the question I have been asked most often. Yes, we will know one another in heaven. However, we will not be sexually motivated in heaven. A woman is not going to bear children and the man is not going to perform the duties of parenting. By no means does the absence of sexuality diminish our personhood. I don't know you in any sexual way; I know you, Dorothy, as a child of God, a fellow pilgrim, a precious servant of the Lord as I enjoy your presence, visiting and sharing with you. That is the way it is going to be in heaven. We will not have children, and we will not live together sexually, but you are going to be you, and I am going to be I, and all other people are going to be they, and we will have the most marvelous happy time together.

Companionship and fellowship are definitely part of God's plan for heaven.

Patterson: **How will we recognize our loved ones and friends? Will we recognize the saints and redeemed of centuries gone by? What about mothers who have lost their babies?**

Criswell: There is a vast amount of knowledge that is intuitive, that is, it is known of itself. On the Mount of Transfiguration, how did Peter, James, and John know that talking to Jesus were Elijah and Moses? They knew it intuitively. By intuitive knowledge we are going to know our loved ones and the redeemed of all ages.

Patterson: **What about the aging process through eternity. Will we hold the age at which we die? Will the baby who dies always be a baby?**

Criswell: Since we are not told, I can only speculate. God will somehow reconcile knowledge and understanding so that we are intuitively known through our souls and spirits and even by our physically transformed bodies. The details of this knowledge are known only to the Lord.

Patterson: **When a loved one dies after the temple in which he lives goes through destructive disease and hurt, will his earthly tabernacle of those last days ever be restored as in the days of health and fullness of life?**

Criswell: According to the Word of God, God will re-create us marvelously and beautifully. I will still be I, and you will be you, but God is going to make us whole and well, complete and fully cognizant of all the goodness of God and riches of His glory. Accordingly, all infirmities will be gone.

Patterson: **Do you think our bodies will take a physical or spiritual shape?**

Criswell: We have an assurance of that in the body of our Lord Jesus. For example, in 1 Corinthians 15, we note the phrase "a spiritual body." The words "spiritual" and "physical" are antithetical—the spiritual or the spirit is contrasted to the physical or the body. The words are confrontational; they are polar opposites. Yet the body that we have is going to be a spiritual body. The Lord could go through a wall or door without opening it; yet He had a physical body. He said, "Touch me and see that it is I myself. Put your finger on the scars, and put your hand in my side." We are going to be that way. Though the body is physical, it will also be spiritual.

Patterson: Thomas Moore, the nineteenth-century Irish poet, had a classic statement about heaven, "Earth has no sorrow that heaven cannot heal." **Do translated saints who have been to heaven know what is going on with those who remain on earth? Will they remember the ones left behind and their problems and hurts? Will they remember loved ones who are lost? If so, how are they going to handle the knowledge that some family members will not go to heaven?**

Criswell: The only reference in the Bible that gives a basis for the thought that the people in heaven are cognizant of things on earth is found following the Hebrews 11 roll call for the great heroes of faith in God's kingdom. "Wherefore seeing we also are compassed about with so great a cloud of witnesses, let us lay aside every weight, and the sin which doth so easily beset us and let us run with patience the race that is set before us" (Heb. 12:1). We can envision the Roman amphitheater and all of those witnesses in the stands, watching the racing of the runners and chariots. The witnesses in heaven looking down upon us are cognizant of what we are doing on earth, but it is not a matter of pain or sorrow to them because there is no pain and sorrow in heaven. These things are all passed away. The Bible says very plainly that all infirmities, sins, and hurts are going to be blotted from our memories and our minds. Our sins are going to be erased from His memory. They are going to be cast into the sea. God is not going to call them to mind anymore. All of the things that will hurt and bring sorrow are gone forever. Perhaps this will illustrate. Suppose my father and mother had reared fifteen children instead of only my brother and me. There would have been thirteen of their offspring about whom I would have no cognizance. They would be nonexistent in my mind. Well, that is the way it is going to be in heaven. Those who are not there will not abide in our memories. However, that does not minimize this ministry of encouragement from the saints in heaven, which is precious indeed.

Patterson: **When we get to heaven, are we going to know** everything about one another, including even those hidden secrets from our earthly lives, or is that personal and comprehensive knowledge confined to God alone? For example, are we going to watch a videotape of our lives, including our darkest moments, when we get to heaven?

Criswell: Emphatically, no! Even God will put that knowledge out of His mind. When we get to heaven, the blood of Christ is going to wash away and blot out all of our sins, and we are going to be pure, spotless, and blameless before the Lord.

Patterson: **We know that we will see Jesus when we get to heaven. But, will we see God the Father, since the Scripture does say that no man has seen the face of God the Father?**

Criswell: I have always preached that there is one God. We know God as our Father; we know God as our Savior; we know God as the Comforter and Encourager in our souls. When you get to heaven, you are not going to see three Gods. The only God you will ever see is the Lord Jesus who became flesh and blood and was resurrected in a human body. The only God you are ever going to feel is the Holy Spirit in your heart, and the only God is God the Father.

Patterson: **Will our relationship to God the Father and to Jesus in heaven be any different than it was on earth?** We have access directly to him, of course, and we can pray and ask him to help us, but I think everyone has gone through a time in his life when he feels that God is just a little beyond reach. **When we get to heaven, is there going to be more accessibility to God, or is it going to be the same type of relationship we have here?**

Criswell: No. Now we see through a glass darkly but then face to face. It is like my listening to you on a telephone and then seeing you face to face or like my reading about you and then getting to meet and talk with you. We are going to have an altogether different relationship in heaven than we have on earth. We are now over here, and He is there; but when we get to heaven, we are going to see each other face to face. We are going to talk together, to visit together, to rejoice together. It is going to be a beautiful relationship.

Patterson: **How is the Christian concept of heaven different from concepts of the afterlife in other religions?**

Criswell: Though we are not going to criticize other faiths, let us focus, for example, upon the Mohammedan's idea of heaven. He sees heaven as a big harem in which he is going to live and indulge his carnal lust with forty women.

The Buddhist's idea of heaven is Nirvana—nothingness. He looks forward to being unmoved and unaware of anything other than mere existence.

The Hindu has an extended vacation between reincarnations, believing that one continues after death to come back again and again.

All of these concepts are different from the Christian faith. A Christian's concept of heaven is that we are going to be with Jesus and with one another; we are going to be perfect; we are going to praise God for His goodness to us world without end.

Our concept of heaven does not have the self-centeredness of other afterlife concepts. We put all of our energies and thoughts toward serving God the Father instead of being concerned about what happens to us.

Patterson: **What will the everyday life in heaven be like?**

Criswell: Paul says, "Eye hath not seen, nor ear heard, neither have entered into the heart of man, the things which God hath prepared for them that love him" (1 Cor. 2:9). That is what life is going to be like in heaven.

Patterson: **Do you think there will be any form of competition among the saints? Do you think Paul and Peter are going to be vying for who is the greatest apostle?**

Criswell: No. We are going to be so in love with the Lord

and grateful to God that we are there that such a thing would never enter the mind.

Patterson: **How about our mobility in heaven?** O. M. Mitchell, the great astronomer, believes that there will be movement back and forth in the galaxies and expresses the determination to go on from world to world continuing his studies in the heavens. **Are we going to flit around from planet to planet—traveling back and forth throughout the heavenlies?**

Criswell: I have a very deep conviction about that. I believe God when He says that He is going to create a new heaven. Not just all of these old burned-out planets and stars—but all of God's creation—are going to be remade. The whole infinitude of God's work is going to be like it was in the beginning before sin destroyed it. Our home will be a mansion in the New Jerusalem, the City of God. From that home we are going to govern God's entire universe. For example, one faithful man is going to be the ruler over ten cities; another faithful man is going to be the ruler over five cities, and God is going to give us assignments according to how we have been faithful in serving Him here on this earth. I've often thought that when we go through space in that new creation and in our new bodies, we will travel instantaneously. I use as an illustration of that how in my mind I can be in Rio de Janeiro right now; then in the next second I can be in Hong Kong, and I can be in Rome or in Paris immediately. In my mind I can be in all those places right now. What I am able to do in my mind, I will be able to do in my spiritual body. It is going to be an inheritance of the whole universe, and we will enjoy it all.

Patterson: **Is there any continuity between the life we live on earth and the kind of life we will experience in heaven? Do you see similarities in the two life-styles?**

Criswell: If you don't like God here, you certainly aren't going to like Him up there. If you don't love the Lord Jesus here, you certainly aren't going to love Him there. The man who doesn't love the Lord Jesus is going to be in torment. All of us who are in the family of God are going to differ just as we do here. There are some of us who just love the Lord, delight to sing his praises, and enjoy hearing his Word preached. There are those who are indifferent. That is the way it will be in heaven. Some of us will be ecstatically happy, and some will just be there and that is all.

Patterson: **Do Christians enter heaven immediately when they die, or do they wait for the return of Christ when the dead in Christ shall rise first?**

Criswell: The Bible is very plain about this teaching. When we die, we go to that intermediate state, the place of the dead (*sheol*, Hebrew; *hades*, Greek). *Hades* is divided into two parts: one part is paradise, and the other part is damnation and torment. The reason for that is not only what the Bible teaches, but it is obvious. We are disembodied spirits when we die, and according to 2 Corinthians 5, we as believers have an abhorrence of disembodiment or nakedness. We want to be whole; we don't want to be a part. When we die, we don't have our bodies, and we have not yet received our rewards. We are just in an intermediate state. At the coming of Christ when we get our new bodies, we will stand at the *bema* (Greek, meaning "judgment seat") of Christ to be given our rewards. It is only then that we enter into heaven.

Patterson: **In this intermediate state, will we immediately be with Jesus?**

Criswell: Yes. The repentant thief was told that he would be in paradise with Jesus on that very day. We go there immediately.

Patterson: **How do you see the difference between the new heaven and the heaven that exists today?**

Criswell: It is the difference between Eden as it was on this earth and the planet earth as we see it today. Eden was a beautiful paradise. Think of the animals and the beauty of life that existed in the Garden of Eden. Yet in the world today there is death and sorrow, pain and heartache, disappointment. All of this has come because of the entrance of sin. That is going to be the difference between this creation that you see and the heaven that God is going to recreate. When God re-creates this universe with the infinitude above and around us, it is going to be Edenic. Every star will be perfect; every planet will be perfect; every part of the universe will be perfect, and we will be perfect in it.

Patterson: **What about heavenly real estate?** Consider this:

Free
Beautiful homes
to be
Given Away
in a
Perfect city!
with
100 percent pure water free
No light bills
Perpetual lighting
Permanent pavement
Nothing undesirable
Everything new
Perfect health
Immunity from accident
The best of society
Beautiful music
Free transportation
Secure a contract today for the new Jerusalem

That sounds pretty good to me! **Are we going to each have our own mansion? Are families going to live together? Will VIPS, i.e., spiritual giants, have bigger and fancier mansions?** *Criswell:* Our homes in heaven will differ just as they do on earth—some large, some small. But every person will be happy because of his ability to appreciate and respond and be sensitive to the grace of God.

Families will be in the same city and in the same wonderful place, but how God is going to distribute us around we will just have to leave to His grace.

Patterson: **Will there be any surprises in heaven?**

Criswell: John Newton, the hymn writer, said, "If I ever reach heaven I expect to find three wonders there: first, to meet some I had not thought to see there; second, to miss some I had expected to see there; and third, the greatest wonder of all, to find myself there."

In Matthew 25, those who were given so much of the grace and goodness of God, as well as these who had nothing and were just cast out, were surprised. I take that as a general review of the whole convocation of heaven. There are going to be many surprises up there.

Patterson: **Can testimonials of after-death-and-returned-to-life experiences be valid in describing heaven, or is the Bible the only reliable source about heaven?**

Criswell: The only way that I know to answer is to say I believe the infallible, inerrant, inspired Word of God, and what the Bible says about heaven I receive with all my heart and soul. Scientists and psychologists have faithfully recorded the testimonies of many who were legally dead and yet reportedly came back to life and described what they had experienced and seen. All I personally can say to that is that it certainly does affirm that there is conscious life after death. When these individuals describe what they have seen and heard, almost always it will be in terms of what the Bible has already revealed. Therefore, I just look upon it as an affirmation.

Patterson: **Will there be humor, laughter, and fun in heaven?**

Criswell: In a recent Gallup Poll, 74 percent responded

affirmatively to that question. I think it is going to be even richer and dearer than what we have known down here in earth.

Patterson: **What are some metaphors or euphemisms used in Scripture for heaven that you think are important?**

Criswell: Everything that is affirmative for the richness of human life would be a beautiful vocabulary to use to describe heaven—the joy of the soul, the happiness of the heart, the cognizance of the mind, the understanding of our hearts, the infinite praise with which we will worship our Lord, the glories of being in a society without hurt or harm or sin or pain or death or suffering. Every good word that is known to the human experience can be used to describe what God has in store for those who love Him in heaven.

Patterson: **Are we going to have work, that is, a job or an occupation, in heaven, or will we spend all our time in a big worship service?**

Criswell: Well, I am sure that we will have a marvelous eternal gladness in the worship of God, but I have always felt that we will have assignments. When our Lord spoke about heaven he spoke of that fellow over there who was so dedicated that he was going to be made a ruler with authority over the people who live in ten cities, and another who would be a ruler over five cities (cf. Luke 19:12-19). When we get to heaven, we are going to have our assignments. I just pray that God will let me have a soap box someplace where I can just preach the Word world without end.

Patterson: **As we talk about what we are going to do, I have categorized some of these heavenly responsibilities, and I want you to comment on each briefly. The first is worship.**

Criswell: Alexander MacLaren said, "The joys of heaven are not the joys of passive contemplation, of dreamy remembrance, or perfect repose; but they are described thus, 'They rest not day or night.' His servants serve Him and see His face." Our worship will be more beautiful and perfect in heaven.

Patterson: **Here you, as a pastor, serve people every day of your life. Do you think that is going to carry over to heaven?**

Criswell: I certainly do. We are going to have things to do and work to accomplish in heaven. Martin Luther once said, "I cannot think what we shall find to do in heaven. No change, no work, no eating, no drinking, nothing to do." Then Melanchthon, his co-laborer, said, "Lord, show us the Father, and it sufficeth us." Then Luther finally responded by saying, "Why, of course, that sight will give us quite enough to do!" In other words, his service was going to be just seeing the Lord. Of course, I would like to take issue with Luther about not eating. What is he going to do when he sits down to the Marriage Supper of the Lamb? Is he just going to sit there? Our service will be, if anything, more extensive and varied.

Patterson: **What do you think about this matter of fellowship as part of our heavenly assignment?**

Criswell: It will be wonderful. What I have come to love and appreciate about others in this life, I will love and appreciate increasingly through all of the eternity that is yet to come. Friendship and fellowship in heaven will be blessed. Archbishop Richard Whately once said, "I am convinced that extension and perfection of friendship will constitute a great part of the future happiness of the blessed."

Patterson: **Will our intellect still be challenged?**

Criswell: Yes. Our vision will be broadened, our appreciation deepened, and our understanding everlastingly expanded. It is going to be wonderful what God is going to make us capable of doing in heaven. We shall understand then, as we do not understand now, what it meant for God the Father to give His only begotten Son.

Patterson: **Will heaven provide a different type of relaxation? How do you see the function of rest as an assignment in heaven?**

Criswell: Of course, in our culture today we think that anything less than constant activity is wasteful. The suggestion has been made that rest in heaven would be different—a rest in knowing, loving, rejoicing, praising. Once in a while at funerals I expound on this unique heavenly rest. Think of the toil and the labor that one who is in pain and sleepless experiences. It is an unbelievable heaviness. But in beautiful rest, you are not in pain any longer; you no longer dread the coming of morning or the falling of night. Think of the rest that you will have in being free from hurt, turmoil, sadness, and pain of body and life. After we have completed an assignment in the presence of God, there will be joy, love, worship, and praise of His name.

Michael Faraday, a chemist, electrician, and philosopher, was asked the question, "Have you conceived to yourself what will be your occupation in the next world?" Hesitating just a moment, Faraday answered, "Eye hath not seen, nor ear heard, neither have entered into the heart of man, the things that God hath prepared for them that love Him." And then he added his own final word, "I shall be with Christ, and that is enough."

We are going to be busy and happy; we will feel useful just being with Christ.

Patterson: **Where did you learn the most about heaven? Was it from the Scriptures, from the books you read when you were preparing sermons, from the seminary classroom, or at the bedside of dying saints? What would you say have been the most valuable lessons you have learned about heaven?**

Criswell: By far I learned more about heaven from the Holy Scripture. Nothing is comparable to what I have learned from the Bible about heaven and about the experience of the human soul's anticipation and preparation for it and liberation to it from the hurt of this mortal body into the glorious likeness of God.

Though the Bible does not provide the answers to all questions about heaven, it does provide the ones we need to know.

Patterson: **Why do some Christians fear death and heaven?**
Criswell: The Lord made us that way. I think God put in us the desire to live, not to die. He put in us a fear of death in order that we would do our work in this life. If there were no fear of death, I'm afraid suicide would be overwhelming. We have a natural human dread for death. The disintegration of the body and its burial conjure up in our minds a frightful and terrible thing, and thus according to the will of God we ought not to live our lives in hope that five minutes from now we will die. Rather, we ought to live our lives in the hope that we will live and serve the Lord for as long as He gives us breath. But the beautiful thing about the Christian faith is that when the time comes for us to die and when our work is finished and the Lord calls us home, then as Christians we ought to sing songs of praise and look forward to seeing Jesus and experiencing the love of God expressed in the beautiful place we call heaven.

Patterson: **What is the most attractive feature about heaven to you? What draws your interest and affection to heaven more than anything else?**
Criswell: The first thing that draws my interest to heaven is just the anticipation of being in the presence of the Lord Jesus, saying something to him, touching him, bowing in his presence, and expressing my love and gratitude for him.

Second, I would love to enjoy reunion with those whom I have loved and lost for a while—the precious members of the family that have gone before me and the host of the dear people from my congregation that I have buried in these more than sixty years as an undershepherd. Oh my, what a rendezvous that will be!

Then, of course, what a wonderful prospect it will be to serve the Lord in heaven—to have an assignment from Him and to do it in His love and grace world without end. What a joy and what a prospect!

Patterson: **When in your many years of ministry have**

you felt closest to the gates of heaven? Was it the time of your plane crash in the Amazon? Was it at the time of your heart attack some years ago? Was it perhaps a time when you have been with a dying saint?

Criswell: I suspect that I have felt more vividly the reality of heaven in some of the high spiritual experiences when heaven came down as I have shared in the congregation of the Lord.

At an Evangelism Conference sponsored by the Baptist General Convention of Texas and held in the Will Rogers Coliseum in Fort Worth, Texas, as I was finishing the sermon on "quench not the Spirit," in the top balcony a preacher began to shout and praise God. He shouted and praised God all the way down from that balcony to the steps of the lower floor, down that long aisle, and finally up on the platform. He put his arms around me, praising God and shouting at the top of his voice. You could not describe that assembly of God's saints even if you had been there to experience it. It was beyond description. It was expressed in a flood of tears. Everyone was crying. It was unspeakable. You just expressed yourself in tears of rejoicing and gladness. In an experience like that heaven comes down.

Well, the opposite occurred one time in the State Evangelism Conference in Hattisburg, Mississippi. When I got through preaching, the Spirit of God was so evidently and powerfully present that nobody moved. It was as though we were trans-fixed. I don't know how long there was silence. Finally and eventually the preacher who was presiding over the meeting stood up and said, "We cannot stay here forever. We must have a benediction and proceed with the work and assignments of the day."

Patterson: Marco Polo, the famous Venetian traveler of the thirteenth century, when he lay dying, was urged by his atten-dants to recant—to withdraw the stories he had told about

China and the lands of the Far East. But he responded, "I have not told half of what I saw."

Whatever heaven is and wherever it is, this much is certain— we shall never be able to tell, not a half, nor even a hundredth part, of what it is like.

PART TWO
What the Bible Says about Heaven
Paige Patterson

CHAPTER 6
Heaven in the Old Testament

The Old Testament is a book of beginnings. Its pages chart the beginnings of our cosmos, the creation of life including human life, the call of a people as a covenant people through whom God would give His precepts to all people. Therefore, the focus of the Hebrew Bible is upon a chosen people and a Promised Land of inheritance to which God would someday deliver them. The concern of these ancient authors was predominantly with initiation and only to a lesser degree with consummation. Occupation of the Promised Land, eviction because of corporate and national sin, and restoration to those sacred precincts is woven into the warp and woof of the Hebrew Scriptures.

Does this mean that the saint of the Old Testament dispensation had no hope of heaven? Was the preoccupation with the land such that it precluded a larger and longer hope? Did the ancients reflect little on the hereafter and the possibility that some aspect of their being would survive and perhaps even thrive in another sphere? There can be no doubt that most of our information about existence after physical death is gleaned from the New Testament. In keeping with an evangelical understanding of "progressive revelation," one should not be surprised to learn more about eternity from Jesus, the "one who inhabits eternity." But this in no sense means that the vision of the prophets was temporally or terrestrially bound. They knew well that they would die, and like almost all other people of antiquity, they believed that something vital survived this earthly sojourn and continued in a different realm. For some, this world to come was a shadowy, ill-defined world of mystery. For others, God gave information at various times that provided encouragement of a sublime state to follow this life.

Heaven, or "the heavens," is mentioned hundreds of times in the Old Testament. In the beginning God created "the heaven and the earth" (Gen. 1:1). The Hebrew word *shamayim,* which is translated "heaven," has at least three senses in the Old Testament. On occasion heaven refers to the atmosphere surrounding the earth. In Deuteronomy 11:11, the wandering Israelites are informed that the Land of Promise is a land which "drinketh water of the rain of heaven." The Lord shall open to them His good treasures including "the heaven to give the rain" (Deut. 28:12). Sometimes God may choose to "shut up heaven that there be no rain" (2 Chron. 7:13) if the children of God are in need of discipline. Birds and eagles fly in the heavens (Prov. 23:5; Gen. 1:26).

At other times all of the intergalactic heavenly bodies are in view. In Genesis 1:15, God places "lights in the firmament of the heaven to give light upon the earth." In Genesis 15:5, God promised that Abraham's descendants would be innumerable like the stars of the heavens. Jeremiah also identified the "host of heaven" that could not be numbered (Jer. 33:22). These luminaries of the heaven are, however, never to be worshipped (Exod. 20:4; Ezek. 8:16). Various heavenly bodies and constellations are specifically named, such as Arcturus, Orion, and Pleiades (Job 9:9; 38:31; Amos 5:8).

Finally, there are those instances where the word clearly depicts another realm, the dwelling place of God and a possible destiny for righteous men (Gen. 5:24; 2 Kings 2:1-18). This third use of the term heaven is the focus of what follows.

When Solomon dedicated the temple in Jerusalem, he spread his hands toward heaven (1 Kings 8:22) and offered a dedicatory prayer, which is no less remarkable for its theological content than for its sincerity. In the process of that prayer the king made two observations about heaven. First, he identified heaven as God's "dwelling place" and asked that God hear from heaven his supplication (1 Kings 8:30). Second, Solomon acknowledged that God could not be contained in heaven since His omnipresence spilled over the brink of eternity and filled all of creation also (1 Kings 8:27). Job apparently recognized heaven as God's "home" and affirmed that his witness and advocate is in heaven (Job 16:19). The Psalmist reminisced that he has no one in heaven to whom he can make appeal other than God (Ps. 73:25) and affirmed that God is seated upon a throne in heaven from which He observes the pitiful rebellion of His creation (Ps. 2:4). Daniel informed Nebuchadnezzar that "there is a God in heaven" who reveals secrets (Daniel 2:28).

But God is not the lone inhabitant of heaven. In Genesis 21:17, an angel of God called to Hagar from heaven. When Jacob fled from his offended brother Esau, he slept under the stars at a place known as Luz. That night in a dream, Jacob observed a ladder extending from earth to heaven, with the angels of God both ascending and descending upon that ladder. Although Isaiah's magnificent vision in chapter 6 of his prophecy is cast against the backdrop of the temple, many interpreters see this as a "heavenly temple" where God's throne is "high and lifted up" and where the angelic order of the seraphim minister around the altar.

But according to the Old Testament Scriptures, do men have the prospect of ascending to heaven? Indisputably, the evidence for ultimate transfer to a heavenly home has greater clarity in the New Testament. But a fair reading of the Old Testament text will also provide abundant evidence for a heavenly abode for the saints. First, there is the evidence found in Daniel 12:2: "And many of them that sleep in the dust of the earth shall awake, some to everlasting life, and some to shame and everlasting contempt."

The passage refers to "many" who sleep (an obvious reference to physical death) and yet who will awake, some to everlasting life and some to everlasting contempt. Whether this refers to a group of people belonging to a certain era (hence "many") or whether it actually includes all who ever live, clearly there is life after death, and one of the options for the continuum of existence is "everlasting life." This is obviously an optimistic prospect, even though the verse assigns no particular location to that existence.

When the first child born to the adulterous union of David and Bathsheba had died, David expressed confidence that, although his child could not be restored, he would go to the child (2 Sam. 12:23). While it may be possible to construe this statement as no more than an admission by David of his own mortality, a much more likely perspective is that David here demonstrates not only a confidence in a life beyond in which knowledge of others continues but also that this life is in a favorable place. It is difficult to see what comfort the king could have derived from the knowledge that he, like his baby, would soon die.

Two of the most helpful incidents from the Old Testament involve the translations of Enoch (Gen. 5:24) and Elijah (2 Kings 2:1-12). In neither case is there even a hint that the disappearance of the man was tantamount to death. "God took him" in the case of Enoch while in the case of Elijah he was taken up "by a whirlwind into heaven." In both instances the implication is that life continues with fellowship in God's presence and, at least in the case of Elijah, with a journey by fiery chariot into heaven. This logically follows since man was made with the capacity to know and experience God. That righteous men should ultimately enjoy the presence of God and the angels is a natural conclusion.

Later Jews understood this Old Testament account of Elijah's translation as a sign that the great prophet continued to live. This is surely a portion of the intent of the transfiguration narrative where Elijah appears on the mountain with Moses (obviously back from the dead!) and with Jesus. There was something unique about the two visitors from the historic past, but they were alive and recognizable. The astonishment of the disciples was not that Moses and Elijah survived death and translation but that they appeared to the disciples. That Elijah had in fact survived was every Jew's affirmation based on the prediction of Malachi, who said:

> Behold, I will send you Elijah the prophet before the coming of the great and dreadful day of the Lord: And he shall turn the heart of the fathers to the children, and the heart of the children to their fathers, lest I come and smite the earth with a curse. (Mal. 4:5-6)

Clearly Malachi, the last of the prophets, had anticipated a ministry of Elijah as a part of messianic promise in the last days. Such would only be possible if Malachi were convinced that Elijah survived death.

Another lesson suggested by the prophecy of Malachi, as well as by the transfiguration appearance, is that the saints survive in a bodily form. The death of the body does not mean that one becomes nothing more than a spirit, an apparition, a ghost. Malachi predicted that Elijah would have a recognizable body, and the gospels confirm that he did appear bodily. But Malachi, the last to take up the prophetic pen, would not have surprised Job, whose story is possibly the oldest written account in the Old Testament. Job directly broached the question of life after death, satisfying himself with the confidence that at an appointed time his "change" would come (Job 14:14), and that, though the flesh were destroyed, he would "see" God upon this very earth (Job 19:25-26). This sighting would be made when Job was once again "in my flesh" (19:26).

Although Isaiah does not mention heaven by that name, the prophet does cite God as saying:

> For thus saith the high and lofty One that inhabiteth eternity, whose name is Holy; I dwell in the high and holy place, with him also that is of a contrite and humble spirit, to revive the spirit of the humble, and to revive the heart of the contrite ones. (Isa. 57:15)

It is interesting that the verse speaks of those of humble and contrite hearts who will join God in the high and holy place where He dwells. Since these "humble" ones are to be "revived," they must be redeemed humans rather than angels.

Elsewhere the Psalms make frequent mention of "the heavens," declaring, for example, that God occupies a throne in heaven from which He observes puny human efforts to resist God and laughs (Ps. 2:4). From this lofty sky-box, God looks down upon and evaluates the sons of man (Ps. 14:2). When necessary, His judgment is "thundered" upon man from His lofty perch (Ps. 18:13). He is just as quick to swoop from His holy heaven to answer the calls of His anointed king in the hour of trouble (Ps. 20:6).

In summary, the consensus of antiquity is that some aspect of human personality survived death. In the religions of the ancient Near East, the concept of a shadowy underworld inhabited by the gods was the destiny of all humans at death. The authors of the Hebrew Scriptures clearly concurred with the judgment that life continues beyond the demise of the body. But from this point on, the biblical picture diverges sharply and provides by contrast not only remarkably precise information about the life to come, but also it adds to such discussions a moral and ethical strain that vastly surpass those of non-revealed faiths.

God is the Creator of the heavens and of the heavens of the heavens. From heaven He reveals Himself and His purposes. Myriads of angels surround Him, serve Him, and rejoice in fellowship with Him and with one another. Because of the devastation of sin, men and women must prepare for death, a universal consequence of sin. But those who have repented and experienced God's gracious forgiveness may anticipate a new life, even a bodily life, in the age to come. The author of Ecclesiastes remarks, "Then shall dust return to the earth as it was, and the spirit shall return unto God who gave it" (12:7). But Job (19:25-27) and Daniel (12:2) anticipate a change or a resurrection that includes the body. The prospect is clearly extended that righteous men will be welcomed to God's abode as sharers of His glory. This ultimate state is not another temporal one but is eternal in its duration. Fear and shrinking are inappropriate for the godly in the face of this prospect so that the Psalmist can quaintly and with pleasant surprise observe, "Precious in the sight of the Lord is the death of his saints" (Ps. 116:15).

CHAPTER 7
The Kingdom of Heaven

No subject received more prominent attention from Jesus than the kingdom of heaven. To have a kingdom, two things are essential—a king and subjects over whom the king exercises hegemony. Though geographical location does not appear essential to the concept of kingdom, it is often closely associated with the idea. The kingdom of heaven, as it is traced on the pages of the New Testament, reflects both possibilities. Sometimes the kingdom of heaven is presented as the acknowledged right and rule of Christ in the human spirit. At other times the eternal residence of the saints seems to be in view. On still other occasions the reference alludes to a kingdom age here on the earth in the last days. Some overlapping of these aspects of the kingdom is noticeable.

In Luke 10:1-16, the seventy are sent to every city Jesus would later visit. Among the other responsibilities was that of announcing that "the kingdom of God is come nigh unto you" (Luke 10:9). A probable understanding of this statement would be that the kingdom comes in Jesus the king and in the opportunity of subjects to respond to Him in faith. Neither the earthly or millennial expression of the kingdom nor, even strictly speaking, the heavenly state is in view here. When in

Mark 12:34 Jesus replied to a questioning scribe, He said, "Thou art not far from the kingdom of God." He did not intend to suggest that the scribe was about to die and enter heaven or that the earthly reign of Christ was about to be inaugurated. Jesus was saying that this scribe was sincere in his queries and thus close to receiving the King, which, in turn, would have placed the scribe "in the kingdom." In fact, Jesus spoke clearly of receiving the kingdom of God as a little child (Mark 10:15), clearly pointing to the fact that one becomes a participant in the kingdom by faith. Jesus also called all men to repentance in light of the fact that the "kingdom of heaven" is near (Matt. 4:17). John the Baptist had already offered the same advice (Matt. 3:2). In all these instances the kingdom is presented as the reign of Christ the king in the hearts of His subjects. The kingdom of heaven is near!

Particularly when Jesus added the prepositional phrase "of heaven" to the discussion of the kingdom, the reference was often to the eternal abode of God and by extension to the holy angels and the saints of God. In Matthew 18:3, Jesus warned that unless conversion occurred, one would never "enter into the kingdom of heaven." In fact, Jesus' contemporaries were told that unless their own righteousness exceeded that of the scribes and the Pharisees, they would "in no case enter into the kingdom of heaven" (Matt. 5:20). To the rich young ruler, Jesus resorted to sacred hyperbole to suggest that it was easier to push a camel through the eye of a needle than to get a wealthy man into the kingdom of heaven (Mark 10:25; Matt. 19:22-23). To Pilate, Jesus indicated that His kingdom was not of this world (John 18:36). All of these references strongly suggest a realm that is extraterrestrial.

That the "kingdom" also has an earthly expression, that which is sometimes called the millennial kingdom, is apparently indicated in passages such as Acts 1:6 when the Lord's disciples ask Him if the time has come for the restoration of the kingdom to Israel. If no earthly manifestation of the kingdom were contemplated, the perfect moment has presented itself for Jesus to correct this erroneous view of the millenium on the part of His followers. Instead, Jesus replied that they neither needed nor would receive knowledge of the time (*chronos,* Greek) or the season (*kairos,* Greek). On other occasions Jesus suggested that the tares would someday be gathered out of His kingdom (Matt. 13:41). In Matthew 8:12, some of the "children of the kingdom" will be cast into outer darkness where there will be weeping and gnashing of teeth. Such expressions would not be appropriate to the ultimate heavenly city where nothing that defiles ever enters (Rev. 21:27). It is also manifestly impossible for the reference to be to the internal reign of Christ in the human heart. Therefore, an earthly aspect of the kingdom must be intended here.

One may safely conclude that there is a sense in which the kingdom of heaven comes to the individual when King Jesus is received and enthroned at conversion. The concept of the kingdom is extended with the dawn of the last days and the rise of the earthly kingdom so often anticipated by the Old Testament prophets. But each of these is only a harbinger of that ultimate and eternal abode wherein only righteousness dwells. This is the city for which Abraham was searching, a city whose builder and maker is God (Heb. 11:10). By studying the parables of the kingdom, we may discern crucial aspects of the kingdom of heaven exhibited to some degree in prior expressions of the kingdom but exponentially enhanced in the final dwelling place of Christ and His saints.

The Hiddenness of the Kingdom of Heaven

Not everyone grasps the nature of the kingdom of heaven. Jesus said to His disciples, "It is given unto you to know the mysteries of the kingdom of heaven but to them it is not given"

(Matt. 13:11). The concept of mystery in religion is almost as old as the race itself. As "mystery" is used in the New Testament, its reference is only to what is knowable as the result of a direct revelatory act of God. Paul speaks, for example, of the Church as a great "mystery" (Eph. 5:32). In other words, none of the prophets foresaw the age of the Church. Almost every other major doctrine embraced in the New Testament was known at least incipiently in the Old Testament. But to the apostles was revealed the mystery of Christ and of His Church.

In like manner the kingdom of heaven is a mystery. Never will it be "discovered" in some research laboratory. Immortality or survival after death may be suspected by philosophers and religious people, but nothing of the nature of heaven—its worship, its occupants, its glories—could be known without the special revelation of God. According to Jesus, this revelation of the mystery of the kingdom of heaven is made only to genuine believers. Others may be taught the language of Zion, but only those initiated into Christ can comprehend a measure of what it all means.

Entrance to the Kingdom of Heaven

Mere vocabulary and even confession of truth will prove inadequate when admission to the kingdom of heaven is sought.

> Not every one that saith unto me, Lord, Lord, shall enter into the kingdom of heaven; but he that doeth the will of my Father which is in heaven.
> Many will say to me in that day, Lord, Lord, have we not prophesied in thy name? and in thy name have cast out devils? and in thy name done many wonderful works?
> And then will I profess unto them, I never knew you: depart from me, ye that work iniquity. (Matt. 7:21-23)

Apparently it is possible to be orthodox but lost. One may have prophesied without regeneration. Others may have fancied themselves to have had a ministry of exorcism only to find themselves excluded from the kingdom of heaven. If such activities do not qualify one for heaven, then how can that celestial home be attained?

First, one arrives in heaven only by invitation. Matthew 22:1-14 chronicles Jesus' parable of the marriage feast. He likens the kingdom of heaven to a king whose son was to be married. Understandably, the wedding, as well as its accompanying feast, would constitute a gala affair, to say nothing of its significance as an official affair of state. As was characteristic of such an ancient Near Eastern event, servants were commissioned to deliver the final invitation to those fortunate enough to be invited. The failure of these ungrateful subjects to respond appropriately became the opportunity for unlikely subjects out on the highways to be invited to the feast. While this parable of the kingdom was primarily designed to demonstrate Jewish failure and the extension of the call of God to Gentile nations, it is also clear that entrance was done on the basis of invitation.

A further feature of this parable is that one might come in response to the invitation but find himself barred from entry if he rejected the attire proffered by the host.

> And when the king came in to see the guests, he saw there a man which had not on a wedding garment: And he saith unto him, Friend, how camest thou in hither not having a wedding garment? And he was speechless.
>
> Then said the king to the servants, Bind him hand and foot, and take him away and cast him into outer darkness; there shall be weeping and gnashing of teeth. For many are called, but few are chosen. (Matt. 22:11-14)

In other words, more than just an invitation appears necessary for entrance into the heavenly kingdom. Just exactly what is required was the subject of the Lord's observation.

Verily I say unto you, Except ye be converted, and become as little children, ye shall not enter into the kingdom of heaven. (Matt. 18:3)

Repent ye: for the kingdom of heaven is at hand. (Matt. 3:2)

Repentance, defined as an acknowledgement of and turning from one's own sinful way as a result of godly sorrow (2 Cor. 7:10) and as a childlike faith leading to conversion are the essentials which qualify one for the kingdom of heaven. The invitation to the kingdom of heaven is the result of grace on the part of the King. The Sovereign even provides the wedding garment. But the potential guest must in humble faith accept both the invitation and the garment of his host.

The call for humility on the party of the subjects of the kingdom of heaven is a recurring theme in Matthew. In the beatitude of Matthew 5:3, "the poor in spirit" inherit the kingdom of heaven. In Matthew 19:14, children are especially encouraged to come to Jesus since individuals who were childlike would make up the kingdom of heaven. By the same token, the rich would find that their pride and independence would make it difficult for them to gain entrance to heaven and more problematic in fact than the task of threading a needle's eye with a surprised camel (Matt. 19:23-24).

Growth of the Kingdom of Heaven

Two of the parables of the kingdom of heaven seem to have been employed by Jesus to forecast rapid and extensive growth. First, the Master compared the kingdom of heaven to the tiny mustard seed which a man might plant in a field (Matt. 13:31-32). In verse 33 of the same chapter the analogy changed to focus a woman who mixed leaven into her dough until thorough permeation was achieved. These are two of the more controversial parables of the kingdom. Interpretations differ widely regarding the significance of each. The central features seem to reflect meager beginnings for the kingdom of heaven, followed by steady growth and ultimately by total permeation. Leaven most frequently represents evil and decadence in biblical analogies. Many interpreters are convinced that the parable of the leaven in the meal features the presence of evil in the earthly expression of the kingdom of heaven. To this writer such explanation seems improbable. The emphasis is rather on the steady growth and mysterious permeation of the kingdom of heaven.

The Value of the Kingdom of Heaven

The intrinsic worth of the kingdom of heaven was emphasized by Jesus in two kingdom parables (Matt. 13:44-46).

> Again, the kingdom of heaven is like unto treasure hid in a field; the which when a man hath found, he hideth, and for joy thereof goeth and selleth all that he hath, and buyeth that field.
> Again, the kingdom of heaven is like unto a merchant man seeking goodly pearls: Who, when he had found one pearl of great price, went and sold all that he had, and bought it.

Here the kingdom of heaven is presented as a treasure, which, when discovered, is recognized to be of such value that it merits the forfeiture of everything else previously possessed by this fortunate prospector. A similar emphasis focuses on a merchant involved in the securing and marketing of costly gems and pearls. One day he comes upon a pearl of such perfect size, shape, radiance, and beauty that he realizes he has discovered the ultimate pearl. Never will he find one superior to this one. Liquidating all else, he purchases this one pearl of great price.

One is not surprised then that Jesus would say in Matthew 6:33 that man should first seek the kingdom of God. The tendency to become attached and devoted to transitory, material objects or to fleeting fame and prestige and in the process miss what is of real value is the concern of these two parables. The value of the kingdom of heaven and the right to be put there is the greatest value. To be a subject of the kingdom of heaven is also to be a recipient of the king's inheritance (Rom. 8:16-17).

The Keys of the Kingdom of Heaven

Subjects of the kingdom of heaven function in responsible roles as citizens of that kingdom. A famous and not infrequently disputed interview of Jesus with Simon Peter serves to exhibit the responsibilities incumbent upon believers. In Matthew 16:13-20 that encounter is recorded. The subject of the encounter was the identity of Jesus. The suggestions as to Jesus' identity offered by some were obviously in error. Then Peter made his avowal that Jesus was the long-awaited Messiah and also "the Son of the living God." Commending Peter for his insight and declaring that insight actually to be the product of divine inspiration, Jesus next spoke of a role which Peter would play.

Peter and, by extension, the whole church would be given the keys of the kingdom of heaven. An accurate translation of Matthew 16:19, reflecting the Greek verb tenses employed, would read,

And I will give you the keys of the kingdom of heaven: and whatever you bind on earth shall have been bound in heaven: and whatever you loose on earth shall have been loosed in heaven.

Whatever the interpretation of this verse, this much is obvious. Subjects of the kingdom of heaven are to be responsible, not just in the hereafter, but also in the present age. The "keys" probably represent the gospel of Jesus the King through which the believer exercises the admitting role into the presence of the King through his faithful rehearsal and unfolding of the truth of the gospel.

The Dawning of the Kingdom of Heaven

The parables of the kingdom of heaven also anticipate a day of reckoning which will inevitably come. The parables of the wheat and tares (Matt. 13:24-30) and of the net (Matt. 13:47-50) cogently illustrate this point. The parable of the tares combines two concepts of the kingdom of heaven, notably the general reign of Christ in the lives of the saints and the inauguration of the final heavenly kingdom. Jesus framed the parable by calling attention to a farmer who sowed good seed and an enemy who clandestinely and furtively sowed his field with weeds. Both are allowed to progress side by side until "the time of harvest." At that point the tares are separated and burned, while the wheat is gathered into the farmer's barn.

The parable of the seine is similar. The kingdom of heaven is compared to a net dragged through the sea, yielding a diversified catch. The bad fish are jettisoned while the good are preserved. Jesus was very specific about the significance of this parable, concluding that at the end of the age angels would "sever the wicked from among the just." The wicked in turn would be cast into a furnace of fire where there would be wailing and gnashing of teeth.

In both parables the idea of the continuance of the present age, sporting its mixture of wickedness and righteousness, is suddenly halted by the intervention of a day of judgment. This includes an identification and a separation of the subjects of the kingdom. In each case the good is preserved in the keeping of the King.

Further Words about the Kingdom of Heaven

There remain at least two interesting comments concerning the kingdom of heaven. The first is the reference of Jesus to a scribe who is instructed in the kingdom of heaven (Matt. 13:52). This scribe is compared to a householder who brings from his treasury things both new and old. This observation follows the query of Jesus about the understanding of His other parables of the kingdom. The disciples are apparently viewed as scribes who were both copiers and interpreters of the law. As scribes of the kingdom of God, they would rehearse old truths and unveil new truths to those who would hear.

The nobility of this labor in behalf of the kingdom of heaven is assessed in Matthew 19:12 during Jesus' discussion of marriage and divorce, in which He noted that some men are made eunuchs at the hand of man, while others "have made themselves eunuchs for the kingdom of heaven's sake." Almost certainly those thus recognized have not mutilated themselves. Neither is this an argument for asceticism or celibacy as being desirable over marriage. Jesus does recognize that some Old Testament prophets, such as Jeremiah, devoted themselves so totally to the work of God that they did not marry. The same would be the case for the apostle Paul at a later date. The saying is apparently intended to stress that marriage is not essential for the one who would proclaim the kingdom of heaven.

Conclusion

The emphasis of Jesus in the parables of the kingdom of heaven establishes a clear concern on His part that the disciples reflect deeply on what it means to be a subject of the kingdom of heaven. This included both recognition of responsibilities in the present age and essential preparation for the end of the age when the final forms of the kingdom of heaven would become manifest. The "already" and "not yet" tension in Jesus' doctrine is a tension which should characterize healthy church life today, maintaining hope for the future and ministry for the present.

CHAPTER 8
The Worship and Work of Heaven

If heaven is a place of eternal rest, then how can there be work in that celestial realm? In the next chapter, the concept of the Sabbath rest will be more fully investigated. For now it is sufficient to say that there is no contradiction at all. Furthermore, the Scriptures describe heaven as a place of the most intense and invigorating activities and adventures. Those activities take two principal forms—worship and service. More is said about the worship of heaven than about the work of heaven, but information is provided about the latter sufficient to stir sanctified imaginations.

The Work of Heaven
The labor of heaven appears in the Scriptures under the rubric of service and sovereignty. In Revelation 7:14, John the apostle has spied an innumerable multitude from every nation standing around the throne of God in heaven clothed in white robes. One of the twenty-four elders engaged the startled apostle in conversation by asking if John could identify this multitude. If John had a clue, he wisely suppressed any hypothesis of his own by deferring to the elder, saying, "Sir, thou knowest." The elder then explained that these were people who came out of the great tribulation having washed their robes in the blood of the Lamb. Concerning their delightful

destiny, he added: "Therefore are they before the throne of God, and serve him day and night in his temple: and he that sitteth on the throne shall dwell among them" (Rev. 7:15).

Another glance into the city of God is accorded the reader in chapters 21 and 22 of the Apocalypse. As John described the amenities of heaven, he noted: "And there shall be no more curse: but the throne of God and of the Lamb shall be in it; and his servants shall serve him" (Rev. 22:3).

In both of these passages the word translated "serve" is the Greek term *latreuo,* which carries a somewhat distinctive emphasis from the prevalent *douloo.* The latter word is often associated with the prevailing practice of slavery in Roman times. As employed by New Testament authors, particularly Paul, the term has lost its objectionable nuances and is transformed into the idea of enthusiastic and voluntary service to Christ through which the "servant" demonstrates his full acquiescence to the lordship of Christ. *Latreuo,* on the other hand, is a word often associated with and frequently translated by "worship." But this is not a passive worship of someone merely observing the activities of others. Originally the noun form *latron* meant "reward" or "wages." Thus, the concept of profitable service emerges. The connections with sacrifice and prayer are also strong. In Romans 12:1, Paul called for the presentation of the body as a "living sacrifice," which he said is our "reasonable service" (*logiken latreian,* Greek) or "logical service."

There is, therefore, no surprise to find this word describing the activity of heaven, particularly in relation to the activity of heavenly worship. Whatever may be involved in this service, clearly fatigue is not engendered since the unnumbered multitude "serve him day and night." The service is clearly both voluntary and spontaneous, arising doubtless from the gratitude to God in the hearts of the citizens of heaven. The tasks are not onerous but fulfilling. The challenges are stupendous but without possibility of failure.

Another activity of heaven is variously described as "reign-ing," "ruling," or "exercising authority." Twice in Revelation 20, verses 4 and 6, there is indication that the saints reign with Christ. Admittedly, in these passages the time of this rule is that period which is generally designated as the millennium or kingdom age on the earth. Elsewhere, however, the New Testament seems to suggest that this "rule" is extended beyond the millennium era. For example, in Matthew 25:21-23 at the conclusion of the parable of the talents, Jesus said: "His lord said unto him, Well done, thou good and faithful servant: thou hast been faithful over a few things, I will make thee ruler over many things: enter thou into the joy of thy lord."

The same promise is given to him who received only two talents and had doubled them. In Luke 19:17 the promise of Christ is made in terms of authority specifically over ten cities. "And he said unto him, Well, thou good servant: because thou hast been faithful in a very little, have thou authority over ten cities."

This parable of the kingdom of heaven suggests an end-time reckoning with an assignment of reward. In a later chapter, we will deal specifically with rewards. Note here, however, that there is strong suggestion of responsibility, authority, and sovereignty. The mention of "cities" may be metaphorically or literally interpreted, but it remains apparently certain that at the end of this present sojourn the saints will be given authoritative assignments involving a certain amount of derived sovereignty.

Someone has defined "sanctified imagination" as the use of the mind to contemplate possibilities as long as those possibil-ities in no way violate the Scriptures and as long as we differ-entiate clearly between them and the facts of the Bible. If someone asks, "Over what shall we be appointed rulers?" we must honestly say that we can only conjecture. As long as it is "sanctified conjecture," we might risk noting that our planet earth is one of the smaller planets. It revolves around only an average-size sun in a relatively small solar system, marooned as it is on the far edge of one of the millions of galaxies in a universe so immense that we fathom part of it only by radio telescope and part of it—perhaps the larger part—not at all! What is the purpose of all of this? If one accepts biblical theism as true and the creation accounts of the Bible as accurate, then it must be the case as Paul says: "For by him were all things created, that are in heaven, and that are in earth, visible and invisible, whether they be thrones, or dominions, or principalities, or powers: all things were created by him, and for him" (Col. 1:16).

Now if everything that exists is the product of God's creative genius, if it is "for" Christ that all things exist, and if the saints of God inherit all things with our elder brother Jesus Christ, then it may not be too much to suppose that all of this incredible unexplored universe will yet have a purpose and a relationship to us that we do not now appreciate. Of course, it is also possible that what we call "heaven" is a realm that so far transcends the bounds of grandeur of the present cosmos as to render our universe inconsequential by comparison. Whichever is the case, the parallels of the kingdom and the description of service in heaven make lucid that there is copious, though never onerous, work in heaven.

The Worship of Heaven

No subject generates any greater excitement for the child of God or more abject boredom for an unbeliever than that of the worship of heaven. Sometimes even Christians fail to grasp the invigorating picture of the worship of heaven, interpreting the possibilities for worship as little more than an extension of what happens in a particular local congregation on Sunday morning at 11:00 A.M. As for the unregenerate, if the songs of Zion, the contemplation of the Word of God, a walk with

Christ in the gardens of prayer, and the fellowship of the saints are not precious here below, it will come as no surprise that little anticipation could be engendered for such experiences on an eternal basis in the hereafter.

Glimpses of heavenly worship appear in the Old Testament in places such as Isaiah 6, where antiphonal shouts of angelic messengers pay homage to the holiness of God. The most extensive insights into heaven's worship are unveiled in the book of Revelation. The first of the spectacular heavenly scenes is described in chapter 4 and involves the combined worship of the twenty-four elders and the four living creatures, usually identified by interpreters as angelic beings. This scene is extended when the Lamb, who is simultaneously the Lion of Judah, steps to the center of the apocalyptic stage. In 7:9-12, the great multitude coming out of the Tribulation joins the praise of God. In 14:1-3, the heavenly orchestra and the 144,000 of Israel's redeemed inaugurate a new triumphant anthem, the lyrics of which only they are privy. In 15:1-5, a song is found extolling Moses and the Lamb. Finally, in 19:1-10, all of heaven appears to pick up the refrain of the melody of triumph. The characteristics of this worship are as follows.

Ascription of Praise

The recurring theme of heavenly worship is praise to God. Sometimes this praise is borne on the vehicle of a shout (Rev. 5:12; 7:10; 19:6), occasionally in melodious song (Rev. 14:3; 15:3), and sometimes with instrumentation (Rev. 14:2). Those who equate reverence with silence may have a surprise in heaven if these passages depict the worship of that heavenly gathering. The shouts of the hymns of heaven reverberate through eternity with certain consistent themes.

First, gratitude to God for who He is and for what He has done in His redemptive work is uppermost in the minds of the redeemed. Therefore, the four living creatures do not rest day or night as they cry, "Holy, holy, holy, Lord God Almighty, which was, and is, and is to come" (Rev. 4:8). They are joined by the twenty-four elders who, casting their victor's crowns before the throne, say: "Thou art worthy, O Lord, to receive glory and honour and power: for thou hast created all things and for thy pleasure they are and were created" (Rev. 4:11).

Specifically in this passage, God is praised for His creative artistry. Glory, honor, and power are particular attributes that God is said worthily to possess. To these are added blessing, riches, and wisdom (5:12-13). The four living creatures echo a cogent "amen" (5:14) to the adulation of the twenty-four elders. "Amen" is an anglicization of a Hebrew word originally carrying the sense of certainty, conviction, or belief. For example, in Jonah 3:5, the people of Nineveh responded to the prevailing of a subdued Jonah in that they "believed God" and repented. The word translated "believed" is *aman*. The "amen" of the living creatures is their affirmation and confession of agreement with all the preceding praise of God.

Gratitude to God for the atoning sacrifice of Jesus is another major motif in heaven's praise. Not only is this a major theme, but also it is one of the elements that distinguishes the book of Revelation from almost all other apocalyptic literature. In 5:9, the twenty-four elders are in view: "And they sung a new song, saying, Thou art worthy to take the book, and to open the seals thereof: for thou wast slain, and hast redeemed us to God by thy blood out of every kindred, and tongue, and people, and nation."

The praise here centers on the worthiness of Christ to open the seven sealed books. Nothing could be clearer than that this worth is predicated upon a redemption purchased through the shed blood, the sacrificial death of the Lamb of God in behalf of the twenty-four elders. Those thus redeemed are not limited to Israel alone. The extension of Christ's saving atonement beyond the pale of Judaism is cause for abundant thanksgiving. In addition, the Lamb is praised for the consequences of His atoning work. The recipients of the benefits of the atonement are also through that medium made kings and priests before God.

In 15:3, the saints of the Tribulation sing an interesting aria, the song of Moses the servant of God and the song of the Lamb. This unique carol linking Moses and Jesus the Lamb not only recognizes the atonement of Jesus but by linking it with Moses also demonstrates that the substitionary death of Christ was always God's plan prophesied even by Moses.

Another feature of the benediction of heaven is the recognition of God's justice and judgment. Although no Christian could rejoice in the condemnation of a person, joy is in order whenever the evil systems of this world are judged and Satan defeated. This explains the heavenly spectacle recorded in chapter 15. Seven angels have appeared bearing seven bowls of the wrath of God. These are about to be placed out on a rebellious world and specifically upon the kingdom and person of the Antichrist. The result is that the residents of heaven who never succumbed to the deceit of Antichrist break into song:

> Great and marvellous are thy works, Lord God Almighty; just and true are thy ways, thou King of saints. Who shall not fear thee, O Lord, and glorify thy name? for thou only art holy: for all nations shall come and worship before thee; for thy judgments are made manifest. (Rev. 15:3-4)

The king of the saints is honored in this song for the justice and truth of His ways. Those just and true ways are about to be exhibited in the outpouring of the wrath of God. This display of God's holiness is especially worthy of the applause of all heaven. In fact, "holiness," which has been described as the single most encompassing attribute of Deity, focuses on the idea of separation and distinction. Justice, even when sought by the purest of men, is always tinged with human fallibility. But God is separate and transcendent from man—His justice is flawless and His judgment is perfect.

The spontaneity, enthusiasm, and emotion of this heavenly revival is apparent in 4:10-11 and in 19:1-10. Victor's crowns are one of the rewards of heaven. But 4:10-11 notes that:

> The four and twenty elders fall down before him that sat on the throne, and worship him that liveth for ever and ever, and cast their crowns before the throne, saying, Thou art worthy, O Lord, to receive glory and honour and power: for thou has created all things, and for thy pleasure they are and were created.

Even the rewards of these elders are obviously viewed as tributes to the grace of God. As a result, the elders whisk their crowns from their heads and cast them before the feet of the Lamb as a paeon of praise. In chapter 19, the whole of heaven is enveloped in the recognition of God's suzerainty. Consider this heavenly scene.

> And after these things I heard a great voice of much people in heaven, saying, Alleluia; Salvation, and glory and honour, and power, unto the Lord our God: For true and righteous are his judgments; for he hath judged the great whore, which did corrupt the earth with her fornication, and hath avenged the blood of his servants at her hand. And again they said, Alleluia. And her smoke rose up for ever and ever. And the four and twenty elders and the four beasts fell down and worshipped God that sat on the throne, saying, Amen; Alleluia. And a voice came out of the throne, saying,

Praise our God, all ye his servants, and ye that fear him, both small and great. And I heard as it were the voice of a great multitude, and as the voice of many waters, and as the voice of mighty thunderings, saying, Alleluia: for the Lord God omnipotent reigneth. Let us be glad and rejoice, and give honour to him: for the marriage of the Lamb is come, and his wife hath made herself ready. And to her was granted that she should be arrayed in fine linen, clean and white: for the fine linen is the righteousness of saints. And he saith unto me, Write, Blessed are they which are called unto the marriage supper of the Lamb. And he saith unto me, These are the true sayings of God. And I fell at his feet to worship him. And he said unto me, See thou do it not: I am thy fellowservant, and of thy brethren that have the testimony of Jesus: worship God: for the testimony of Jesus is the spirit of prophecy. (19:1-10)

Here almost every element and every constituent of heaven is incorporated in the doxology. The great voice of an enormous multitude is heard shouting, "Alleluia." This adulation is the result of the judgment of God on apostate and false religion (the great whore), for the just reign of the Lord God omnipotent, and for the fact that the church—the wife of the Lamb—has made herself ready. She is arrayed in radiant white purity, the righteousness of the saints.

On occasion most of us have found ourselves standing in the midst of a throng at a Billy Graham Crusade or another gathering of a host of God's people. Many times I have been present at the annual pastors' conference of the denomination to which I belong. More than twenty-five thousand people stand and, as a heavenly choir, sing "How Great Thou Art." I can seldom sing. I try, but as often as not, I find myself so deeply moved at this corporate praise of the Jesus who saves us that I can only stand and quietly praise Him with the hot tears of my eyes and the inward testimony of gratitude in my heart.

If one can be so deeply affected by such an earthly gathering housed in a relatively unattractive convention center with songs marred by all of the imperfections of humanity's best effort, I can only begin to comprehend heavenly worship. Imagine the whole church of God, the saved of all time, Old Testament and New Testament saints, myriads of magnificent angels, musicians with trumpets, harps, assorted other instruments, and in the midst the Lord Jesus arises from the throne. Moses, Elijah, Abraham, David, Paul, John, and others fall before Him in adoration. The blasts of the trumpets shake the foundations of hell, and the sweet strains of the consoling harps remind the saints that they are home. Shouts of alleluia and amen punctuate the crescendo of the heavenly choir, while angels shout in the background, "Holy, holy, holy, Lord God Almighty." There are Jews and Arabs with arms locked in an embrace of love. African-Americans and Anglo-Americans stand beside Japanese and Koreans. The common feature of gratitude to Christ for His saving grace has knit them all together. Millions now sing the song of Moses and the Lamb. Such a scene can only encourage those who have His holy name. We are moved to say with John, "Even so, come, Lord Jesus!" (Rev. 22:21).

CHAPTER 9
The Concept of the Sabbath Rest

Historically, the Jewish people have attached significance to the fourth commandment, which has been accorded in some regards more importance than any others in the decalogue. Only the commandment relating to the Sabbath is repeated in one form or another with such frequency in the Old Testament, appearing in Exodus 20:8-11; 23:12; 31:12-17; 34:21; 35:1-3; Leviticus 19:3; 23:1-3; 26:2; and Deuteronomy 5:12-15. Such prominence is demonstrable also over the interpretation and observance of the law of the Sabbath in the conflicts of Jesus with the Pharisees.

It is not surprising that the author of Hebrews proposes that "there remaineth therefore a rest [*sabbatismos*, Greek] to the people of God" (Heb. 4:9). In fact, the first eleven verses of Hebrews 4 seize the idea of the Jewish Sabbath and relate it to heaven in a remarkable way. But in order to understand the author's use of this idea, we must begin with the Old Testament and continue through the development of the concept in later Judaism.

Judaism was not entirely alone in its concept of the Sabbath. Holy days were celebrated in about every ancient faith. A remarkable parallel exists, however, among the Babylonians. There the seventh, fourteenth, twenty-first and twenty-eighth

days of the months *Elul* and *Marcheshwan* required the observation of certain rules. These mandates included prohibitions
for shepherds, such as forbidding them to cook flesh on coals
of fire or eat it or bake bread on the Sabbath. Neither could the
shepherd wash his clothes on those hallowed days. The king
was not permitted to mount his chariot or to speak as ruler. A
physician was not to lay a hand on a patient until the day had
passed. At the place of the mystery (the Babylonian Mysteries)
one viewing the sacrifices was compelled to do so in absolute
silence. Some of the days carried the name *shappath,* the precise
meaning of which is not known. However, its phonic similarity
to the Hebrew *shabbath* is interesting, to say the least.

In Judaism the Sabbath legislation is outlined formally in
Exodus 20:8-11:

> Remember the sabbath day, to keep it holy. Six days
> shalt thou labour, and do all thy work: But the seventh
> day is the sabbath of the Lord thy God: in it thou shalt
> not do any work, thou, nor thy son, nor thy daughter,
> thy manservant, nor thy maidservant, nor thy cattle, nor
> thy stranger that is within thy gates: For in six days the
> Lord made heaven and earth, the sea, and all that in
> them is, and rested the seventh day: wherefore the Lord
> blessed the sabbath day, and hallowed it.

Notice first that the purpose of the Sabbath is that it be
kept holy unto the Lord. Holiness is always contrasted with
the profane or common. In contrast to the other six days of the
week, this Sabbath day was to be set apart and devoted to the
things of God. While it is true that *shabbath* means "rest" in
Hebrew, a misunderstanding of that "rest" not only led the
Jews seriously to err in their application of the law but also
has led Christians to misunderstand the nature of heaven as a
rest for the people of God. The notion of the Sabbath as a

siesta or a day of total inactivity is foreign to the word.

The Sabbath is historically linked to the days of God's creation of the cosmos. In six days the Lord made the heaven and the earth. On the seventh day He rested and hallowed the day forever. Not germane to this discussion is the question of the length of the creative day, though the application of the creative week to the Jewish week can be said to favor the idea of the days of creation as being actual twenty-four hour periods. In any event, it goes without saying that God was not exhausted by His six days of labor in creating the cosmos. Quite to the contrary, one can only be struck by the simplicity of the creative acts of God, which were accomplished to a large degree by simply calling things into existence. Since no recuperative rest is required for God, it seems safe to conclude that the historical account calls our attention rather to the fact that upon completion of creation God turned to other activities somewhat in the same way a concert pianist might say, "I will rest from my practice and work for awhile in my garden."

Interestingly, the commandment mandates six days of labor and in so doing not only forbids indolence but also dignifies to the point of religious importance the notion of meaningful labor or work. What is forbidden in the statute is not activity but rather common activity of the variety pursued on the remaining six days. Instead "the seventh day is the sabbath of the Lord thy God." The Sabbath is to be devoted specifically to the things of God, to spiritual reflection, renewal, service and worship. And this Sabbath is to be a perpetual ordinance (*berith olam*, Hebrew) between God and His people (Exod. 31:16).

In this latter sense, the Sabbath also serves as a sign (Exod. 31:13, 17) between *Yahweh* and Israel. Therefore, an almost evangelistic nuance may be discerned in the statute. Fires were not to be kindled (Exod. 35:3) nor trade carried on (Neh. 10:31). The solemnity of this commandment presents itself with clarity to the reader in the incident recorded in Numbers 15:32-36. A man was discovered gathering sticks on the Sabbath, presumably to build a fire. Brought before Moses, The man was isolated until Moses could ascertain from God what ought to be done with the offender. "And the Lord said unto Moses, the man shall be surely put to death: all the congregation shall stone him with stones without the camp" (Num. 15:35). The participation of the whole congregation in the execution of the penalty for this capital crime was designed to stress not only that such sentences were to be carried out only by the community alone but also to focus universal attention on the holiness attached to the Sabbath legislation.

Not only was there a Sabbath day, but also a sabbatical year was ordained of God. In Exodus 23:10-11, Moses recorded the following:

And six years thou shalt sow thy land, and shalt gather in the fruits thereof: But the seventh year thou shalt let it rest and lie still; that the poor of thy people may eat: and what they leave the beasts of the field shall eat. In like manner thou shalt deal with thy vineyard, and with thy olive yard.

At the end of the seventh sabbatical year, the Jews were also to observe the Jubilee (Lev. 25:8-55). This fiftieth year or Jubilee saw the proclamation of liberty to all inhabitants of the land who, for whatever reason, had become slaves. In that year, just as in the sabbatical year, the land was allowed to lie fallow. Inheritances sold to others were returned to the original family owners in the Jubilee year. All of these ideas have significance in the ultimate Sabbath of rest which we call heaven.

By Jesus' day, rabbinic efforts to comprehend the significance of the Sabbath had become complicated to the point that they had forfeited much of the original meaning, allowing Sabbath to become a burden rather than a blessing. The same remains true even in modern Israel where, for example, some hotels have Sabbath elevators. Since it is wrong to work by pushing a floor indicator, the elevator is programmed to stop on every floor. On the Sabbath one only hopes there is no emergency demanding quick access to one's hotel room on the nineteenth floor!

Lists in the Jewish *Mishnah* prohibited forty tasks minus one. Creative Jews were industrious enough to locate an assortment of loopholes in this legislation; so the rabbis expanded these thirty-nine prohibitions with their own six interpretations of each. Thus more than two hundred Sabbath prohibitions came to prevail. The tasks of "knowing" the prohibitions was almost as onerous as the necessity of abiding perfectly by such interpretations. And these interpretations did gradually assume the force of the commandment itself.

From the Sabbath controversies between Jews and Jewish legalists, help is available for constructing an idea of what the final Sabbath of rest will be. One of the earliest of these confrontations materialized when the disciples of Jesus plucked ears of wheat on the Sabbath. The story, which is recorded in Matthew 12:1-8, notes that the Pharisees remonstrated with Jesus about the Sabbath-breaking behavior of His followers. At this point, Jesus appealed to the Scriptures, citing the action of David's entry into the Holy Place in order to eat the showbread. Jesus was making the point that sustaining life was more important than maintaining ceremony. He concluded this dissertation with the astonishing affirmation "For the Son of man is Lord even of the sabbath day." Aside from this rather obvious assertion of deity, Jesus is saying something critically important about the Sabbath—any Sabbath, including the final rest. The Sabbath is not an end in itself but is itself subject to the sovereign Lord. Heaven's Sabbath, as refreshing as it is, is invigorating precisely because it is that realm in which God's reign is perfect.

Another conclusion is a part of Mark's account of the same incident. In Mark 2:27, Jesus observes that "The sabbath was made for man, and not man for the sabbath." This idea removes all of the objectionable features of legalism from the Sabbath and views it as an ordinance designed to enhance the quality of human life. By the same token, the final Sabbath of rest has been carefully "prepared" (John 14:3) for the benefit of the children of God.

The meeting with the man whose right hand was withered, recorded in Luke 6:6-11, provides still an additional insight into Jesus' view of the Sabbath. Scribes and Pharisees doubtless sensed that the compassionate Jesus could not bypass this helpless fellow. Knowing that this was the Sabbath, they could accuse him of violating the law of Moses if He healed the man. Aware even of their thoughts (here one sees the omniscience of deity), Jesus said, "I will ask you one thing; Is it lawful on the sabbath days to do good, or to do evil? to save life or to destroy it?" (Luke 6:9). Then He healed the man's hand. Clearly then the Lord of the Sabbath made the Sabbath for man, and the Sabbath existed for the doing of good and for the saving of life. In all of these respects, the final Sabbath rest closely parallels the Sabbath of Moses' code. Additionally, such an insight prepares us to comprehend the extended analogy of heaven as Sabbath as found in Hebrews 4:1-11 (italics mine):

> Let us therefore fear, lest, a promise being left us of entering into his rest, any of you should seem to come short of it. For unto us was the gospel preached, as well as unto them: but the word preached did not profit them, not being mixed with faith in them that heard it. For we which have believed do enter into rest, as he said, *As I have sworn in my wrath, if they shall enter into my rest;* although the works were finished from the foundation of the world. For he spake in a certain place

of the seventh day on this wise, *And God did rest the seventh day from all his works. And in this place again, If they shall enter into my rest. Seeing therefore it remaineth that some must enter therein, and they to whom it was first preached entered not in because of unbelief: Again, he limiteth a certain day, saying in David, Today, after so long a time; as it is said, Today if you will hear his voice, harden not your hearts.* For if Jesus had given them rest, then would he not afterward have spoken of another day. There remaineth therefore a rest to the people of God. For he that is entered into his rest, he also hath ceased from his own works, as God did from his. Let us labour therefore to enter into that rest, lest any man fall after the same example of unbelief.

This passage is a warning that not all enter in to the rest of God. In fact, the possibility of "coming short" of that rest ought to inspire fear, according to the author of Hebrews. A strong allusion remains like a warning drum beating in the distance. This allusion is to the failure of the children of Israel to enter the Promised Land from Kadesh Barnea. Having experienced the undeniable hand of God at the crossing of the Red Sea, even including God's destruction of Pharaoh's army, the Israelites faltered at Kadesh when ten of the twelve spies expounded upon the superiority of the Caananites.

Two results followed. First, God announced that for the next forty years they would wander the Sinaitic wastes until the corpses of this generation fell in the wilderness. Second, upon hearing this disturbing prospect, the presumptuous decision was made to go up immediately to conquer the land, whereupon that generation got a good start on the prophesied carnage in the wilderness—being defeated thoroughly by the enemy. Every Jew knew this history by heart. Now the author of Hebrews reminds his readers that the same tragedy could repeat itself.

Avoiding such a calamity could be achieved only by faith. The gospel is true, regardless of its reception. In order for those who hear it to enter into rest, the preaching must be received, "being mixed with faith." There are two options. Those who do not mix faith with the gospel are excluded from the heavenly rest. Exclusion, however, is not the worst of it. Citing Psalm 95:11, the author of Hebrews notes that this prohibition is the result of God's having sworn in His wrath that they should not enter His rest. The strong Greek term *orge* is invoked to describe the settled and unchangeable character of God's animosity toward sin.

But if some must be excluded, the good news is that "some must enter therein" (Heb. 4:6). The rest, which the vagabonds of Sinai experienced upon entry into the land of Canaan under Joshua (4:8), was not the ultimate rest, as only a cursory reading of Joshua and the other historical materials will show. Since that "rest" of Joshua had its limitations, "There remaineth therefore a rest (*sabbatismos*, Greek) to the people of God" (Heb. 4:9). Everywhere else in this passage the Greek word for "rest" is *katapausis*. In 4:11, the character of this rest begins to be clearly delineated by the change from the general *katapausis* to the very specific *sabbatismos*.

This sudden change signals an identification of the anticipated ultimate Sabbath with all of the Sabbath legislation of Israel. Just as the sacrifices of the Levitical system pointed inexorably down the halls of history to the ultimate sacrifice, the Lamb of God that takes away the sin of the world, so the Sabbath, the sabbatical year, and the years of Jubilee were poignant advertisements of a final rest yet to come. Just as the Sabbath was not a mere siesta, so the Sabbath rest of heaven should not be construed as an experience in which the glorified saint becomes a "cloud potato," reclining as he polishes harp and halo throughout the aeons of eternity. Rather the heavenly sabbatical is described precisely in 4:10 as an experience in which the regenerate man has "ceased from his own works, as God did from his."

Just as God's rest is not recuperative but rather a substantive change in the nature of His activity, so the eternal rest of the believer consists of laying aside the "labor" of this life, together with its exhausting effects, and replacing it with new, invigorating activities which produce neither weariness of body nor boredom of mind. This coming rest is a repose of discovery, adventure, learning, worshipping, rejoicing, and ruling. It recaptures the loss of Eden's paradise and much more besides. This is the ultimate Sabbath for which no further rest will ever be sought or needed.

The author of Hebrews concludes his treatment with a final admonition in verse 11 to labor now to enter into that rest. This is not a proposal for some sort of "works salvation" or a threat of possible apostasy. Rather, the author desires that his hearers respond with the essential faith to secure the Sabbath of God and then diligently to labor below, knowing that this happy repose awaits each believer. Here on earth there is an obnoxious aspect, a debilitating aspect of our labor even under optimum conditions. The eternal Sabbath stands in colorful and inviting contrast to this pilgrimage.

CHAPTER 10
The Inhabitants of Heaven

In the introduction, I mentioned the presidential primary when Dr. James Kennedy questioned each of the candidates. Everyone running for the office said that he definitely intended to go to heaven. Most people do. But most people will not go to heaven!

That shocking observation is not popular these days. The superciliously, syrupy, sweet order to which we have evolved finds such a thought distasteful. In the movie *Crimes and Misdemeanors,* Woody Allen rehearsed a murder in which the felon apparently escapes detection and justice. The movie implied that there is no justice or judgment at a later time either. Jesus clearly had another perspective. He warned:

> Enter ye in at the strait gate: for wide is the gate, and broad is the way, that leadeth to destruction, and many there be which go in thereat: Because strait is the gate, and narrow is the way, which leadeth unto life, and few there be that find it. (Matt. 7:13-14)

Jesus' declaration that few enter the way to eternal life while many go to destruction is in stark contrast to the confidence of contemporary man. Nor is heaven to be composed of those who are religious as opposed to those who are not. "Not everyone that saith unto me, Lord, Lord, shall enter into the kingdom of heaven" (Matt. 7:21), cautioned the Lord. In fact, Jesus recognized that in the day of judgment there would be those seeking heavenly asylum on the basis of such activities as exorcism of demons and other miracles performed in Christ's name (Matt. 7:22-23). These also would be turned away. These "children of the kingdom" would be cast into outer darkness where they would experience only weeping and gnashing of teeth (Matt. 8:12). Who precisely are these who are excluded?

The concluding chapters of the Apocalypse address the question of eternal reward and everlasting retribution. In Revelation 21:8, John wrote:

> But the fearful, and unbelieving, and the abominable, and murderers, and whoremongers, and sorcerers, and idolaters, and all liars, shall have their part in the lake which burneth with fire and brimstone: which is the second death.

Obviously there are those who have committed all of those heinous offenses who do arrive in heaven. Therefore, even though not explicitly stated in this verse, the reader is to understand that unrepentant murderers, adulterers, idolaters, etc. who have not conquered through the blood of the Lamb (Rev. 12:11) will find themselves confined to the lake of fire. If someone protests that he is guilty of none of these offenses, he only needs to note that those who are "unbelieving" are also condemned.

In Revelation 21:27, John provided an even more comprehensive basis for judgment: "And there shall in no wise enter into it any thing that defileth, neither whatsoever worketh abomination, or maketh a lie: but they which are written in the Lamb's book of life."

Here there are three specific exclusions followed by a general one. Since the inheritance of the saints is "incorruptible and undefiled and . . . fadeth not away" (1 Pet. 1:4), anything that would defile, deceive, or be an abomination would introduce imperfection to that perfect realm. God is "of purer eyes than to behold evil, and canst not look on iniquity" (Hab. 1:13); no presence of evil is allowed to penetrate the heavenly kingdom. There follows a reference to the Lamb's Book of Life. In chapter 20 of the Revelation, a search has been made in the Lamb's Book of Life. Those whose names are not included, regardless of status in the present age, are cast into the lake of fire.

Unfortunately, the only conclusion conceivable is that those who are blood-bought sinners whose names are entered in the Book of Life are saved while all others are forever excluded. This was not God's design for man. The everlasting fires of hell were prepared for the devil and his angels (Matt. 25:41), but God is so gracious that He never coerces anyone to be the object of His affection and adore Him. If there is rejection of His overtures, then the only option is the place called hell. Tragically, this is the destiny of most.

This is not to say that heaven will not be thoroughly populated. The throne room vision of Revelation 4, with its notable similarities to Isaiah's vision in chapter six of that prophecy and Daniel's introduction to the Ancient of Days in Daniel 11:1-6, focuses on the central figure of heaven, the risen, glorified, and exalted Lamb. Consider these descriptions of the One who occupies that throne:

> And immediately I was in the spirit: and, behold, a
> throne was set in heaven, and one sat on the throne.
> And he that sat was to look upon like a jasper and a

sardine stone: and there was a rainbow round about the throne, in sight like unto an emerald. (Rev. 4:2-3)

In Revelation 1, the Son of Man is thus described:

And in the midst of the seven candlesticks one like unto the Son of man, clothed with a garment down to the foot, and girt about the paps with a golden girdle. His head and his hairs were white like wool, as white as snow; and his eyes were as a flame of fire; and his feet like unto fine brass, as if they burned in a furnace; and his voice as the sound of many waters. And he had in his right hand seven stars: and out of his mouth went a sharp twoedged sword: and his countenance was as the sun shineth in his strength. (Rev. 1:13-16)

As coming King and invincible Warrior, John describes him as follows:

And I saw heaven opened, and behold a white horse; and he that sat upon him was called Faithful and True, and in righteousness he doth judge and make war. His eyes were as a flame of fire, and on his head were many crowns; and he had a name written, that no man knew, but he himself. And he was clothed with a vesture dipped in blood: and his name is called The Word of God. And the armies which were in heaven followed him upon white horses, clothed in fine linen, white and clean. And out of his mouth goeth a sharp sword, that with it he should smite the nations: and he shall rule them with a rod of iron: and he treadeth the winepress of the fierceness and wrath of Almighty God. And he hath on his vesture and on his thigh a name written, KING OF KINGS, AND LORD OF LORDS. (Rev. 19:11-16)

As reigning and implacable Judge, according to John, he sat upon the Great White Throne, and his countenance was such that the earth and the heaven fled away, yet there was found no place of concealment from his gaze (Rev. 20:11).

Combining these descriptions, heaven must be an incomparable place with no presence other than the glorified Lord. His white hair suggests both antiquity without aging and holiness. His piercing eyes penetrate beyond any subterfuge and know all things. Bronze feet reveal His omnipotence. His voice reverberates like a thousand mighty cataracts on a raging river. Small wonder John was overcome and fell at His feet as though dead (1:17).

The apostle's attempt to describe the radiant color of the throne room vision of chapter 4 seems to exhaust the potentials of human language. As the Warrior King of chapter 19, heaven's Conqueror is viewed by John as riding a white steed adorned with a robe dipped in blood.

He is draped with descriptive names, Faithful, True, The Word of God, and one cryptic name which only the Lord Himself could comprehend. Heaven's host follow in the attire of imputed righteousness. Out of the Warrior King's mouth flicks a sharp sword, and He shepherds the nations with a rod of iron.

If this poignant description suffers the limitations of human discourse, it is nonetheless sufficient to reveal the focus and most important inhabitant of the kingdom of heaven. To the lost He is terrifying. To the redeemed He is enthralling. To all He is awesome.

Joining the glorified Lord in heaven will be the angelic hosts. Those who do not take the existence and activity of angels seriously have a problem with the Scriptures. Angels appear in the narrative of Scripture early as guardians of the garden from which our first parents were evicted in Genesis and appear with increasing frequency throughout the Bible.

An angel announced to Mary and to Joseph the impending birth of Jesus, shouted His nativity to astonished shepherds, and assured startled apostles that this same Jesus who was taken into heaven would come again in the same manner of His departure.

What are angels anyway? Why do they sometimes have two wings (Exod. 25:20), sometimes four (Ezek. 1:6), sometimes six (Isa. 6:2), and, on occasion, no wings at all (Gen. 18)? Why is it that humans sometimes see angels (Acts 27:23), while under other circumstances, they are apparently unseen visitors (1 Cor. 11:10)? The key to these questions is provided by the author of Hebrews in 1:13-14, as he references Psalm 110:1. Angels are spiritual beings created by God. They may apparently assume whatever form is necessary, although it is also possible that different orders of angels simply have distinct appearances. Two orders of angels are specifically mentioned, the cherubim (Gen. 3:24) and the seraphim (Isa. 6:2).

Responsibility for these angelic beings is "to minister for them who shall be heirs of salvation." Although they are unable experientially to fathom the redemptive grace of God (1 Pet. 1:12), their assignment of ministry to the heirs of salvation is varied. In addition to the heralding tasks associated with the birth of Jesus, angels strengthened Jesus in Gethsemane (Luke 22:43), stood sentinel at the empty tomb to announce the Lord's resurrection, and gently chide the disciples for seeking the living among the dead (Luke 24:5). Angels can be formidable pugilists, as Peter learned when awakened in prison by a sharp jab to the side from the hand of his rescuing angel (Acts 12:7). In need of wisdom and in danger from man and nature, Paul testified that an angel appeared to him aboard ship in the midst of a boisterous sea and assured him of the safety of all (Acts 27:23). In one of the most enigmatic passages of the New Testament women are told that when the church assembles they are to have authority on their heads because of the angels

(1 Cor. 11:10). Whatever this means it at least seems to suggest unseen angelic messengers attending worship with the saints. Finally, one may even be surprised to entertain angels, unaware that his visitors are of heavenly origin (Heb. 13:2).

If angels are prominent in the affairs of this age, then heaven is replete with their activities. In the throne room visions in Revelation 4, there are four beasts, better translated "living ones" (*Zoa*). They possess multiple sets of eyes and have the sequential appearances of a lion, a calf, a man, and a flying eagle. Each has six wings. They need no rest but indefatigably repeat the refrain "Holy, holy, holy, Lord God Almighty, which was, and is, and is to come" (4:8). This signals the beginning of the response of the twenty-four elders.

Identifying these living ones might have proved elusive had it not been for the appearance of almost identical spirits in Ezekiel's visions. There are differences, but the similarities outweigh the peculiarities. Ezekiel says flatly, "This is the living creature that I saw under the God of Israel by the river of Chebar; and I knew that they were the cherubims" (Ezek. 10:20). Thus we are introduced to these cherubim who seem to serve as the facilitators for the worship of heaven.

Angels continue to dominate the landscape of the book of Revelation. A strong angel cries in a loud voice seeking someone worthy to open the seven-sealed book in the hand of God (5:2). Angels restrain the hurricane velocity of the winds of God's wrath until another angel can seal the 144,000 Jews who are saved during the debilitating days of Daniel's seventieth week (7:1-8). Angels' blasts herald the "trumpet judgments" (chapters 8–9), and angels overturn the bowls of God's wrath as the final judgments of God during the Tribulation period (chapter 16). An angel speaks with John on more than one occasion, as, for example, when he calls the apostle's attention to the judgment of the great whore (17:1).

An angel is involved in the peculiar incident recorded in

chapter 10 of the Apocalypse. Here a spectacular angel appears with a little book in his hand. John is instructed to make an approach to the angel and request the book. When he does, the angel instructs him to eat the book. The description of it sounds like a dish from a Chinese restaurant—sweet and sour. The book was sweet in John's mouth but bitter in his stomach. He is then told that he must yet bring this bittersweet message of God to many people and ethnic groups—a remarkable promise and commission for a man who may well have been a centenarian by this time. Finally, an angel lays hold upon Satan and chains him in the abyss for one thousand years (20:1).

Angels once again appear in the vision of the heavenly capital recorded in Revelation 21 and 22. Like a celestial real estate agent, one of the angels who had poured out the bowls of wrath approaches the beloved disciple and offers to show him the bride, the Lamb's wife (21:9). Twelve angels were posed as sentinels at the twelve gates of the New Jerusalem (21:12). The remainder of the tour is conducted by this angel. John is so impressed with this radiant guide that he prostrates himself in an act of worship. This becomes the occasion for a gentle rebuke. In appealing humility, the angel forbids this worship and explains: "See thou do it not: for I am thy fellowservant, and of thy brethren the prophets, and of them which keep the sayings of this book: worship God" (Rev. 22:9).

Finally, the angel instructs John not to seal the contents of the book he has received. The "time" (*kairos*), meaning God's choice of moment, is said to be near, and the message of the book is to be made known.

Angelic spirits are then prominently present in the activities and worship of heaven. These are joined by the saints of God from the Old Testament period. In the intriguing story which Jesus told in Luke 16:19-31, the beggar named Lazarus dies and is immediately met by angelic beings who ferry him to "Abraham's bosom" (16:23). Later in torment the rich man asks that Lazarus be sent to cool his parched tongue (16:24), and still later, that he be allowed to approach the wealthy merchant's five brethren back on earth (16:27-28), ostensibly because the added evidence of the return of someone from death would be more convincing. "Abraham's bosom" is a Hebraism, which clearly describes a place where Abraham and the other Old Testament saints are domiciled. It is a place of comfort (16:25), a place where possible encroachment is prohibited by a great gulf (16:26), and a place, by implication, where there is great joy and fulfillment. Lazarus joins Abraham, alive and alert, aware both of his own status and that of the damned also. This appears to take place within moments of Lazarus' demise, thus ruling out any prospect of so-called "soul sleep." This accords well with the promise of 2 Corinthians 5:8, where we are informed that "to be absent from the body" is "to be present with the Lord."

The appearance of Moses and Elijah on the Mount of Transfiguration seems to suggest that these esteemed characters from Israel's past were alive, active, free from any kind of incarceration, and marvelously mobile. Therefore, the reader of Revelation 4 is not surprised to find present in the throne-room vision twenty-four elders. These elders are reposing on twenty-four thrones. They are attired in white clothing, an indication of holiness. This description could just as well cause the interpreter to see them as some of the leadership of the myriads of heavenly angels. But then they are further said to have on their heads crowns of gold. These crowns are not diadems but victor's crowns (*stephanoi*). Angels are never depicted on the pages of the Bible as occupying thrones or as wearing victor's crowns. The most likely conclusion is that these elders represent the redeemed people of every era. There are twelve patriarchs of Israel and twelve apostles of the Lamb. Both Old Testament saints and those from the church age are present in heaven.

No more beautiful or comforting passage is found in the Bible than the precious promise of Jesus recorded in John 14:1-5. Jesus had begun the process of preparing the disciples for His departure and subsequent absence of now almost two thousand years. Although Jesus explains this as necessary for the coming of the Holy Spirit (John 16:7), sensing uncertainty and sorrow at the announcement of His departure, He offers these words of encouragement:

> Let not your heart be troubled: ye believe in God, believe also in me. In my Father's house are many mansions: if it were not so, I would have told you. I go to prepare a place for you. And if I go and prepare a place for you, I will come again, and receive you unto myself; that where I am, there ye may be also. And whither I go ye know, and the way ye know. (John 14:1-4)

The promises here are several. First, there is the promise that Jesus is going to the "Father's house," where there are already many dwellings. The disciples will eventually arrive there also. Thus Jesus is preceding them to prepare a place for them. Jesus Himself will come again and receive them to Himself and abide with them eternally. The way to the Father's house is already known to the disciples because Jesus is the way, the truth and the life (John 14:6).

Paul eagerly anticipated this coming of the Lord but knew that death might overtake him first. Paul described this experience of physical death as the dissolving of our present tent (2 Cor. 5:1). He preferred to be clothed with a "house which is from heaven" so that he would not be found "naked" (2 Cor. 5:2-3). The "house which is from heaven" is doubtless a reference to the glorified body to be received at the return of Christ. The state of "nakedness" to which the apostle referred suggests a disembodied condition, which is the state of the Christian between death and the return of Christ. As indicated earlier, this does not mean "soul sleep," for to be away from the body is to be present with the Lord.

In that heavenly city, "the nations of them which are saved" walk in the radiant effulgence of the city (Rev. 21:24). These have eternal access to the tree of life (Rev. 22:14) and live forever in a state of incomparable bliss. But are there other forms of life in heaven? People often ask about the destiny of favorite pets. The Scriptures are silent. Since only humanity carries the image of God and thus the capacity to survive physical death, the answer is almost certainly that the family pet Spot will not be there. But if on earth God is a God of such creative variety as we see exhibited in the animal kingdom, why should that creative genius not be even more spectacularly represented in heaven? Perhaps numberless fascinating life forms are present in heaven. Who knows?

What is clearly apparent is that the Lord is there with His holy angels and saints from both Old and New Testament epochs. This alone is enough. Consequently, the book of the Revelation concludes with an evangelistic invitation: "And the Spirit and the bride say, Come. And let him that heareth say, Come. And let him that is athirst come. And whosoever will, let him take the water of life freely" (Rev. 22:17).

CHAPTER 11

The Splendors of Heaven

Comfort in this age is provided by the indwelling presence of the Holy Spirit. While that comfort is altogether adequate, it constitutes only the beginning of that which may ultimately be anticipated by the believer. Paul discussed this idea in the heart of the second epistle to the Corinthians: "Now he which stablisheth us with you in Christ, and hath anointed us, is God; Who hath also sealed us, and given the earnest of the Spirit in our hearts" (2 Cor. 1:21-22).

The Holy Spirit constitutes an "earnest payment." An earnest is not, however, a mere down payment; rather it is an initial installment, which guarantees the eventual payment of the whole. In this case, the "earnest" is an inheritance held for every believer in heaven. Elsewhere, Paul described this inheritance more comprehensively.

> For as many as are led by the Spirit of God, they are the sons of God. For ye have not received the spirit of bondage again to fear; but ye have received the Spirit of adoption, whereby we cry, Abba, Father. The Spirit itself beareth witness with our spirit, that we are the children of God: And if children, then heirs; heirs of God, and joint-heirs with Christ; if so be that we suffer with him,

that we may be also glorified together. For I reckon that the sufferings of this present time are not worthy to be compared with the glory which shall be revealed in us. For the earnest expectation of the creature waiteth for the manifestation of the sons of God. For the creature was made subject to vanity, not willingly, but by reason of him who hath subjected the same in hope, because the creature itself also shall be delivered from the bondage of corruption into the glorious liberty of the children of God. (Rom. 8:14-21)

A number of features characteristic of this inheritance are herein enumerated. First, the apostle observed that his "reckoning" (*logizomai*), a bookkeeping term meaning "to account," reveals that whatever sufferings one must endure in the present age are unworthy of comparison with the glory which will someday be unfurled. A moment's consideration of the chronicles of Paul's own sufferings in various of his letters and in Luke's history in Acts, to say nothing at all of the long wasting imprisonments, tortures, hardships, and martyrdom of the people of God in every era, is sufficient to impress any sensitive heart with the weightiness and significance of those sorrows. Paul insisted that these are simply unworthy of comparison against the coming glory. If the sufferings and martyrdom of the saints glow like a small light bulb against the backdrop of sin and evil, that is, the darkness of this age, then when the glory of the Sun of Heaven arises, darkness leaps on its fastest steed and flees altogether. Indeed the prophetic John observed, "And there shall be no night there" (Rev. 22:5).

The precise nature of this glory begins with the renovation and recreation of the natural order, which, as depected by Paul, "groaneth and travaileth in pain . . . until now" (Rom. 8:22). This fallen natural order will be delivered from its corruption

(8:21), a promise reflected by Jesus in a frequently overlooked promise in Matthew 19:28.

> And Jesus said unto them, Verily I say unto you, That ye which have followed me, in the regeneration when the Son of man shall sit in the throne of his glory, ye also shall sit upon twelve thrones, judging the twelve tribes of Israel.

The word translated here "regeneration" (*paligenesia*) is used in the entire New Testament only here and in Titus 3:5. In Titus 3:5, the reference is clearly to personal regeneration or rebirth which occurs at the moment of genuine repentance toward God and faith in Jesus Christ. However, in the Matthew passage, the word refers to cosmic regeneration, an eschatological event presaged by Peter also in 2 Peter 3:10-13.

> But the day of the Lord will come as a thief in the night; in the which the heavens shall pass away with a great noise, and the elements shall melt with fervent heat, the earth also and the works that are therein shall be burned up. Seeing then that all these things shall be dissolved, what manner of persons ought ye to be in all holy conversation and godliness, looking for and hasting unto the coming of the day of God, wherein the heavens being on fire shall be dissolved, and the elements shall melt with fervent heat? Nevertheless we, according to his promise, look for new heavens and a new earth, wherein dwelleth righteousness.

Along with the renovation of the cosmos, another glory of heaven will be the glorified body of the individual believer. Paul spoke of our own groaning within as we await adoption, which, he said, is the "redemption of our body" (Rom. 8:23). This same hope, obviously precious to the apostle, is discussed in some detail twice more in 1 Corinthians 15 and in 2 Corinthians 5. In this latter passage, Paul described that heavenly body as a "building of God," an eternal home in heaven made without human hand (2 Cor. 5:1). That body is said to be an immortal body incapable of death, "swallowed up of life" (5:4).

In 1 Corinthians 15, this missionary-statesman provides a lengthy apology defending the resurrection of Jesus from the tomb. Based on the fact of the resurrection and the nature of Christ's glorified body, Paul inferred the nature of the believer's glorified body. This body is said to be a spiritual body as opposed to the natural body which we now have (15:46). This is not to suggest that this "spiritual body" is only a "spirit" with no material reality. When Jesus met Mary Magdalene in the garden following His resurrection, she fell before Him and held Him. Jesus had to say, "Mary, stop clinging to me." Clearly she had hold of something substantive. The glorified body of Jesus was real. In the Upper Room, He ate fish and a piece of honeycomb. These did not fall to the floor but were apparently digested. His body was real, but different, since He also walked through locked doors without opening or disturbing them in any way.

Further contrasts between natural and glorified bodies are that natural bodies are "sown in corruption," while glorified bodies are incorruptible; present bodies are sown in dishonor and weakness but raised in glory and power (15:42-43). One of the splendors of heaven will be a powerful, incorruptible, and honorable body that will be immortal. No longer bound by the space-time continuum, the resurrected body will through all eternity be a living testimony to the redeeming act of God in Christ.

Most of the remaining splendors of heaven are delineated by John in the Apocalypse. But before leaving the testimony of

Paul, one other astonishing text merits attention. In 2 Corinthians 12:1-10, there occurs an important assessment of human suffering revolving around Paul's thorn in the flesh. This malady, the precise nature of which remains unknown, was given the apostle following a remarkable experience in which Paul spoke of being "caught up" into the third heaven. The Greek word translated "caught up" is *harpazo*, which is the same word employed in 1 Thessalonians 4:17 to describe the sudden transfer of believers to the presence of Christ at His return. The word often refers to the action of a thief who quickly absconds with another's property.

In just such a manner, Paul was caught away to the third heaven, the unique dwelling of God. This place he further described as paradise, a Persian loan word originally referring to a beautiful garden or oasis. Once there he heard unutterable words which were "not lawful for a man to utter" (2 Cor. 12:4). This expression does not seem to suggest any known law of God or man. He just means that what he heard, viewed, and experienced defied description and that, in any event, he was forbidden to speak of them.

Two consequences derived from this experience. First, he was given a thorn in the flesh to prevent pride from developing as a result of the abundance of revelation which he enjoyed (12:7). The second consequence was a total metamorphosis of Paul's attitude toward suffering. In light of what he knew of paradise, he was actually able to take pleasure in infirmities and even glory in these (12:9-10). Every hopeful Christian probably finds himself wishing that Paul could have shared at least a glimpse. In a sense, he did. Just to say that one's attitude toward suffering was so monumentally transformed by this vision, to say that a thorn had to be inserted to prevent pride and guarantee humility is to say that this paradise must have exceeded Paul's fondest expectation of the life and city which lay on the other side.

Toward the end of the first century, the pastor of the congregation of Christians assembled at Ephesus was incarcerated by Roman imperial authorities in a barren rock quarry about twenty-five miles out into the eastern Aegean Sea. The island's name is famous today as Patmos, a pretty, horseshoe-shaped island with a crystal blue bay, trees, rows of white dwellings, and a monastery on the high place. In John's day, it was hardly so salubrious. The aging John was also caught up into heaven (Rev. 4:1) and saw at least a portion of what Paul had observed earlier. There was one difference. In part, John was allowed to share his vision for all to know. Glimpses of heaven occur throughout the book, such as in 1:12-18; 4:1-11; 7:16-17. Major focus on the splendors of heaven awaits the readers in the book's concluding chapters 21 and 22. Our attention will also be riveted primarily upon these texts.

Scholars have differed radically from one another as to exactly what it is that John described in Revelation 21–22. This variance, together with the poverty of human language to provide adequate definition to these glorious visions, should engender more than just a degree of interpretive caution. Nevertheless, the broad lines of something not of this age are clearly enough in view. Perhaps what emerges in the New Jerusalem of this text is the equivalent of heaven's capital city. There are many other questions about heaven that simply cannot be determined from these accounts.

For example, where is the geographical location of heaven? Jesus ascended up into heaven, but was this simply an accommodation to assist the disciples by drawing their focus to the permanent departure of Jesus and to prepare them for the advent of the Holy Spirit? Is heaven up somewhere in intergalactic space? Or is it totally outside the bounds of the universe? Or perhaps, since it is a spiritual realm, heaven actually exists concomitantly with the physical cosmos in something of the same fashion time warps are imagined. We do not know. The Scriptures are silent on these issues.

The picture is not even clear about the location of the New Jerusalem, the capital of heaven. Some commentators believe it is to be suspended above the millennial earth. Others imagine that it is suspended above the new earth. Again all of this amounts to sanctified speculation since the text simply does not specify those answers and seems to be unconcerned about even asking such questions.

But if some questions about the Holy City must be bracketed to await the future, some things about heaven can be determined from these two chapters. First, this city belongs to the new order because the first heaven and the first earth have passed away (21:1). Just as Jesus promised in John 14:2-3, the Holy City, New Jerusalem, descends from heaven "prepared as a bride adorned for her husband" (21:2). The most important feature of the city and its most exquisite splendor is that "the tabernacle of God is with men," and God now visually dwells among them (21:3). In the person of the Holy Spirit, He has always been among His children, never leaving them as orphans (John 14:18). But this unseen presence of God meant that we walked by faith and not by sight. Now sight is added to the glory of heaven.

Announcing that the one sitting on the throne makes all things new, John mentions among these "new things," new conditions. God wipes away all tears. Death, crying, pain, and sorrows have perished: "the former things are passed away" (Rev. 21:4-5). God perpetually satiates the thirst of His saints with a fountain of the water of life (21:6). Not only does the Lord quench the thirst of His redeemed, but also He introduces them to their incredible inheritance, for they "shall inherit all things" (21:7). The verse poignantly suggests that heaven is in part what every believer inherits.

Then an angel, who had formerly been a harbinger of wrath, invited John to follow and observe the bride, the Lamb's wife

(21:9). As John stood atop a mountain observing the descent of the dwelling place of the church, he first observed that in the general character of the city, there was a radiant sparkle which reminded him of a jasper stone. The glory of that sparkle was clear like crystal.

Next the reader is introduced to the portals of the heavenly city. Twelve gates guarded by twelve angels are inscribed with the names of the twelve tribes of Israel (21:12-13). The symbolism here may be a reminder that entrance to heaven for all of the nations comes through God's chosen people, the Jews— the nation through whom the Messiah came. The gates are evenly distributed with three facing each of the four directions. Later in verse 21, John revealed that each gate is made of one incredible pearl. The pearl is a gorgeous gem that is created as an oyster responds to the discomfort of a lodged grain of sand. In an appropriate sense then the gates of entrance are pearls reminding the reader that the splendor of redemption arose out of the hurt of sin.

Twelve distinct foundations form the underpinning for this heavenly metropolis. These contain the names of the twelve apostles of the Lamb, since the Christian faith is constructed "upon the foundation of the apostles and prophets" (Eph. 2:20). Each of these foundations is garnished with precious stones. "Garnished" (*cosmeo*) is the word from which the English term *cosmetics* is derived. The essential meaning is "to adorn." The rich adornments of the foundations of the walls of the city sparkled with precious stones.

The difficulty of precision in identifying all of the stones mentioned was forcefully impressed upon me when I sought to construct for my wife on our twenty-fifth wedding anniversary a "heavenly bracelet" with pearl latchets, gold band, and the twelve gemstones mentioned (Rev. 21:19-20). Those stones that can be almost certainly identified include the deep blue sapphire (though some think that this is really lapis lazuli), the chalcedony with its milky border and violet center, the startling green of the emerald, the gold-like transparent yellow of the topaz, and the royal purple of the stately amethyst. Less certain but still probable identification can be suggested for the jasper stone, the Greek for which actually means "spotted." It naturally occurs in several colors but probably refers here to a green quartz. Likewise, the sardius stone was apparently a kind of carnelian ranging in color from dark brown to dark red, while the sardonyx was a form of onyx sporting layers of brown and white. The beryl is easily enough identified but comes in such an assortment of colors as to reduce the interpreter to an hypothesis. A bluish-green color is one of the most frequently found colors. A jacinth probably referred to what is now called a zircon, which, though it appears in several colors, probably refers here to the fiery blue sparkling stone.

This leaves only the illusive chrysolite and chrysoprasus stones, which are uncertain. Some suggest that the chrysolite is actually the peridot, which is an apple-green, transparent stone. The chrysoprasus possibly belongs to the quartz group and is also sometimes called chalcedony. This color ranges from almost emerald green to a turquoise shade. This rich sparkling mixture of reds, blues, greens, golds and whites suggests the breathtaking and arresting beauty of this city.

The angel escorting John on the celestial tour then measured the city with a golden reed (Rev. 21:15-17). The length, breadth, and height of the city were all discovered to be twelve thousand furlongs or stadia. This means that the city stretched for fourteen hundred to fifteen hundred miles along each wall and then towered a similar distance into the air. This colossal megalopolis had walls which either were 216 feet wide or perhaps reached a height of that measurement. This wall was like jasper, and the whole city appeared to be transparent gold (21:18).

If John searched for a temple, he was disappointed (21:22).

With the Lord God Almighty and the Lamb present, a temple was not necessary or desirable. Neither was it necessary to have moon or sun, since the Lamb was the light of the city, illuminating it perpetually with the very glory of God. The pearl gates are never shut for two reasons. First, all that could ever defile the city has been confined forever to the lake of fire (20:15). And those who wish to come from there to the heavenly city find that a great gulf interdicts that crossing (Luke 16:26). Second, the open gates suggest that heaven is larger than its enormous capital, the New Jerusalem. Its inhabitants come and go at will, always having access to God.

A final splendor is unveiled as John looks on—one which is recorded at the beginning of the final chapter of Revelation. For those whose lives have been lived primarily outside of desert regions, it is difficult to imagine the refreshing hope and happy repose of this final vision. But for John, the unpolluted river of the water of life, clear as crystal, flowing from the throne of God was as inviting, provisionary, and invigorating as could be imagined. His predicament on Patmos was made like that of Coleridge's Ancient Mariner, "Water, water everywhere and not a drop to drink."

This flowing river nourished a tree-lined boulevard where grew the tree of life, which bare twelve kinds of fruits for the healing of the nations. The trees offered a harvest every month. The Bible begins with man in Eden having access to the tree of life. Following the rebellion of Adam, the first family is exiled from the garden and barred from the tree of life. All subsequent history is a story of consequent death in the human family. But in Revelation 22, John sees the ravages of disease and genetic weakness transformed by the healing leaves of the tree of life.

A paragraph promising the abolition of the curse, the opportunity of the saints to behold the face of the Lamb, along with promises of divine ownership and protection indicated by the presence of the name of the Lamb in the foreheads of His servants, concludes the vision of the heavenly city, the City of God. A thousand questions are left unanswered. Curiosity and even speculation are as it were almost encouraged to abound. Caution, however, must prevail so that no more is stated than can be scripturally supported.

But if questions remain for modern readers, surely they remained for John also. However, even what he had observed was sufficient to provoke the apostle to awe-inspired humility.

> And I John saw these things, and heard them. And when I had heard and seen, I fell down to worship before the feet of the angel which shewed me these things.Then saith he unto me, See thou do it not: for I am thy fellowservant, and of thy brethren the prophets, and of them which keep the sayings of this book: worship God. (Rev. 22:8-9)

CHAPTER 12
The Rewards in Heaven

Eternal life, the presence of Jesus, and heaven itself would be sufficient even if no other rewards were forthcoming in heaven. But the subject of eternal rewards surfaces in the Scriptures with a fair degree of regularity. Important questions concerning these rewards center around the nature of those rewards, the rationale for the bestowal of such rewards, and the use that will be made of them. If distinctions based on greater or lesser rewards are made in heaven among the saints of God, how can equality and happiness be maintained? This last question is rather less worthy than the others, but it is often candidly asked.

Evidence for Heavenly Rewards
In Isaiah 40:10-11, the prophet is instructed to comfort the people of God who have just been informed in chapter 39 of the certainty of coming Babylonian captivity. In addition to the promise of pardon for Jerusalem's iniquities and the hope for the arrival of the Messiah, the further promise is made that when Messiah arrives, He will have His reward with him.

Behold, the Lord God will come with strong hand, and his arm shall rule for him: behold, his reward is with him, and his work before him. He shall feed his flock like a shepherd: he shall gather the lambs with his arm, and carry them in his bosom, and shall gently lead those that are with young. (Isa. 40:10-11)

Although the precise nature of this reward is not defined, the promise is repeated in even more graphic form.

Behold, the Lord hath proclaimed unto the end of the world, Say ye to the daughter of Zion, Behold, thy salvation cometh; behold, his reward is with him, and his work before him. And they shall call them, The holy people, The redeemed of the Lord: and thou shalt be called, Sought out, A city not forsaken. (Isa. 62:11-12)

The general features of the reward promised here are that God's people will be a holy people, a redeemed people, and a people no longer estranged, isolated, and hated, but rather a people sought and desired. Admittedly, these promises of reward could be millennial in nature. Even if that is the case, there is a close relationships between the millennial kingdom and the ultimate heavenly kingdom. As Paul said, "Then cometh the end, when he shall have delivered up the kingdom to God, even the Father" (1 Cor. 15:24). The records then have profoundly permanent and eternal significance.

The expression in Jeremiah 17:10 takes a different approach but the message remains the same. "I the Lord search the heart, I try the reins, even to give every man according to his ways, and according to the fruit of his doings." While many of the promises in the Old Testament are of a temporal and material nature, this affirmation has a distinctly prophetic angle.

The New Testament abounds in promises of anticipated rewards. The concluding beatitude spoken by Jesus gave comfort and assurance for those who are subject to persecution and harassment for the sake of the kingdom of God. These are instructed to rejoice and be exceeding glad, "for great is your reward in heaven" (Matt. 5:12). Several features of this beatitude arrest the contemplative reader. First, the place of receiving these rewards is "in heaven."

This is not to deny that there are "earthly rewards" for the fruitful servant of Christ. Jesus may well have had in mind exactly this when He said of the giving of alms that they should be given in secret, "and thy Father which seeth in secret himself shall reward thee openly" (Matt. 6:4). Neither can it be said that there is anything wrong with rewards given here on the earth.

But there are problems with earthly rewards. They are generally temporal and often tied in some sense to the material world. Heavenly rewards are consequently preferable. Heavenly rewards may not be recognized at all in human time, but they are nonetheless worth the wait. Further, even the smallest and most insignificant gesture in behalf of God's kingdom is not overlooked by God.

> He that receiveth a prophet in the name of a prophet shall receive a prophet's reward; and he that receiveth a righteous man in the name of a righteous man shall receive a righteous man's reward. And whosoever shall give to drink unto one of these little ones a cup of cold water only in the name of a disciple, verily I say unto you, he shall in no wise lose his reward. (Matt. 10:41-42)

Assisting a prophet or a righteous man with so much as a cup of cold water in the midst of a tiresome and hot journey merits for the donor the same reward accorded to the prophet or righteous man. This observation is critically important for two reasons. First, too frequently, individual believers find themselves feeling like second-class kingdom citizens rendered insignificant since they can neither preach, sing, nor play. This statement of our Lord suggests that "support ministries" merit the same rewards as those received by spokesmen and others with "high profile" ministry efforts.

In this regard, it is well to recall the words of Paul concerning the otherwise obscure Onesiphorus. Of him Paul said:

> The Lord give mercy unto the house of Onesiphorus; for he oft refreshed me, and was not ashamed of my chain: But, when he was in Rome, he sought me out very diligently, and found me. The Lord grant unto him that he may find mercy of the Lord in that day: and in how many things he ministered unto me at Ephesus, thou knowest very well. (2 Tim. 1:16-18)

Here is a man who, as far as we know, never preached a sermon, wrote an epistle, or sang an anthem. His quiet efforts to assist the great missionary-statesman and "refresh" him, "ministering" to him in every way possible, merited not only his favorable mention on the pages of Scriptures read by man for now nearly two thousand years, but also Paul's prayer of intercession in his behalf. Doubtless, he also has preserved for him in heaven the same reward as that abundant reward awaiting Paul himself. Regardless of the apparent unimportance or limited recognition granted to a ministry, this promise is to assure us that such efforts are never unnoticed in heaven and further that heaven is where they will ultimately be rewarded (Heb. 6:10).

The second engaging truth from Jesus' promise in Matthew 10:41-42 is that the reward will be both full and satisfying. This confidence enables the believer to approach life from a totally different perspective. According to the author of Hebrews, Moses chose to suffer affliction with the people of God in place of the honors of Egypt. This he did because he was "esteeming the reproach of Christ greater riches than the treasures in Egypt: for he had respect unto the recompence of the reward" (Heb. 11:23-26). Certainly, there were rewards for Moses as leader of Israel. But Moses' career as a Midianite shepherd for forty years would not have landed him in some ancient *Fortune 500* tablet, nor would his experience as scout master of two million troopers for forty years in the Sinai have made any stellar impressions on a biographical resume. Clearly, Moses had to look beyond this life and world. So should modern Christians!

Promises of reward are also found in other apostolic writings. In 2 John, the beloved disciple warns believers not to lose those things which they have produced so that they can "receive a full reward" (verse 8). Such a statement clearly implies not only promise of reward but also degrees of reward or at least a difference between partial and full reward. In the closing chapter of John's Revelation, Jesus spoke, promising a hasty return and adding that "my reward is with me" (Rev. 22:12).

Paul discussed rewards several times. In Ephesians 6:8, the apostle noted that any good thing a believer does will receive a reward from the Lord. In 1 Corinthians 9:17, Paul speaks of the obligatory nature of his task of preaching the gospel. However, he also noted that should he perform this task willingly, he will receive a reward. This brief survey of the evidence for heavenly rewards should be sufficient to demonstrate that such compensations are not contrary to the hope of heaven as revealed on the pages of the Bible. But when are these rewards to be apportioned?

The Judgment Seat of Christ

Every Greco-Roman city of significance and size boasted a *bema*. In the King James Version text of the Bible, the term *bema* is translated "judgment seat," but such a translation may be misleading. In the ruins of ancient Corinth, one of the best examples of a *bema* is preserved. Approaching the city down a street of marble columns, a large raised platform is clearly in view at the termination of this colonnaded street. The Acrocorinth, a towering rocky mountain, protrudes from the middle of the city beyond the *bema*. This *bema* is actually a platform for military and civic review. An army returning from a successful field campaign would parade down the thoroughfare, halting at the *bema* to receive special recognition for valor in conflict. At the conclusion of the famous Isthmian Games, awards for successful competition were sometimes distributed at the *bema*. No other information of importance is provided except that as a part of the event "every one of us shall give account of himself to God" (Rom. 14:12). "For we must all appear before the judgment seat [*bema*] of Christ; that every one may receive the things done in his body, according to that he hath done, whether it be good or bad" (2 Cor. 5:10).

First, it should be noted that the letter is addressed to the Christians in Corinth and not to unbelievers at all. Only believers then appear at the *bema*. Second, the word which is translated "bad" in the King James Version is the Greek word *phaulon,* meaning "bad" in the sense of "worthless." This suggests that the nature of the judgment in view is not that of condemnation or salvation but rather assessment of effectiveness in one's vocation as a Christian.

This nuance of the text seems to be supported by a much lengthier discussion found in 1 Corinthians 3:11-15:

> For other foundation can no man lay than that is laid, which is Jesus Christ. Now if any man build upon this foundation gold, silver, precious stones, wood, hay, stubble; every man's work shall be made manifest: for the day shall declare it, because it shall be revealed by fire; and the fire shall try every man's work of what sort

it is. If any man's work abide which he hath built thereupon, he shall receive a reward. If any man's work shall be burned, he shall suffer loss: but he himself shall be saved; yet so as by fire.

The *bema* is not mentioned here by that name, but a comparison of passages will establish that the event in view is quite distinct from the judgment of the sheep and goats in Matthew 25:31-46 and from the awesome Great White Throne Judgment of Revelation 20:11-15. Further, the similarities between this passage and the brief discussions in Romans 14:10 and 2 Corinthians 5:10 make it almost certain that the episodes delineated are one and the same. The teaching of Paul in 1 Corinthians merely adds detail overlooked in the other passages.

Specifically, the apostle painted an architectural picture. In the life of every born-again child of God a foundation has been laid. That foundation consists of the person and work of Jesus Christ. No other foundation is acceptable. This foundation becomes applicable to any individual when Christ is appropriated by faith. Following this laying of the foundation at conversion, one spends the remainder of his life building a superstructure upon that foundation. No judgment ever takes place regarding the foundation since "he that believeth on him is not condemned" (John 3:18). Instead, the superstructure is assessed when "the day shall declare it" (1 Cor. 3:13). This "day" is apparently a day immediately following the removal of the church from the earth. Every genuinely born-again child of God will appear before the *bema* of Christ.

The basis of assessment is presented in terms of the materials employed by the believer-craftsman in the building of the superstructure of his life. Some construction engages the use of gold, silver, and precious stone. Other efforts make use of wood, hay, and stubble (3:12). The contrast is first between materials which are only rarely found (gold, silver, and precious stone) and materials which normally are in abundant supply (wood, hay, and stubble). Both beauty and limited availability raise the price or value of the gold, silver, and gemstone. Wood, hay, and stubble are common and normally of no great beauty. Some Christians build into the superstructure of their lives valuable virtues which sparkle like gemstones. They are noticeable in part because these virtues are rarely found in significant quantities, even among believers.

The text leaves to our imaginations (or perhaps to our knowledge of other Scripture) the precise nature of the virtues or worthless attitudes and actions described by the two groups of metaphors. Now the fruit of the spirit is love, joy, peace, long-suffering, gentleness, goodness, faith, meekness, and self-control (Gal. 5:22-23). These sound very much like the sort of attitudes and actions which would be of eternal consequence. Elsewhere the Scriptures urge believers to pray "without ceasing" and to study to show themselves approved unto God. Again, we are emphatically commissioned to be witnesses and even ambassadors for Christ. The practice of these disciplines pleases God and surely constitutes the incorporation of gold, silver, and precious stone in the construction of a Christian life.

On the other hand, preoccupation with worldly concerns, such as possessions, prestige, position, and popularity, would qualify as wood, hay, and stubble. These are concerns and commitments which may not constitute heinous sin as such, but they are those attitudes and actions common even to the lost world. They are "worthless." Often public observation of the believer's life will yield little evidence of the presence of those rare virtues which should distinguish Christians from non-Christians.

However, the moment of truth comes when the contrasting

materials of life's building are tested by fire. Wood, hay, and stubble ignite when subjected to fire and are promptly consumed. Gold, silver, and gemstones are not destroyed by the fire but most often only purified by that fire. A day is coming, according to Paul, when the works of believers will be tried and revealed by fire. Note that this is no doctrine of purgatory since it is not the believer but the works of the believer that are tested by fire.

How precisely could this happen? The awesome description of the glorified and reigning Christ recorded in Revelation 1:12-17 describes Christ as one whose "eyes were as a flame of fire" (1:14). Have you ever had the experience of standing before someone of almost impeccable justice and moral character while you misrepresented something? The fabricator under such circumstances will inevitably avoid the eyes of the one who is just. In the same way, as each believer stands before the exalted Lord Jesus, His eyes, like a flame of fire, will penetrate every disguise, revealing all that is present in the hearts of His children. That which has the character of wood, hay, or stubble will be consumed. That which has the character of gold, silver, or gemstone will be purified by the Savior's gaze.

The surviving and purified virtues are then counted as reward in the heavenly kingdom. Those whose works are burned shall suffer loss, but they themselves are saved "yet so as by fire" (1 Cor. 3:15). Two observations are critical. First, the crucial necessity is that of being saved. Reward or loss of reward notwithstanding, everyone in heaven will know what he has received and what he has escaped by the grace of God and will, therefore, be supremely happy. Second, there is no good reason to approach the *bema* having built with inferior and vulnerable materials. Rather, every child of God in gratitude to God for his salvation should labor incessantly to build virtues that engender permanent reward.

The Nature of Rewards in Heaven

Rewards in heaven are almost certainly infinitely more diverse and fulfilling than anything we can contemplate. The Scriptures provide just enough information to whet our spiritual appetites. At least two distinct categories of reward are discernible in the Bible. First, there are the rewards of responsibility. Finally, there are the rewards of adornment. Even these latter rewards of adornment have a pragmatic function, as we shall discover.

Luke 19:11-27 (similar to the parable in Matthew 25:14-30) records what has been called the "Parable of the Ten Pounds." One of the general teachings of this parable is that those who are faithful in assigned spiritual tasks in this life will be rewarded by increased authority in the age to come.

> And as they heard these things, he added and spake a parable, because he was nigh to Jerusalem, and because they thought that the kingdom of God should immediately appear. He said therefore, A certain nobleman went into a far country to receive for himself a kingdom, and to return. And he called his ten servants, and delivered them ten pounds, and said unto them, Occupy till I come. But his citizens hated him, and sent a message after him, saying, We will not have this man to reign over us. And it came to pass, that when he was returned, having received the kingdom, then he commanded these servants to be called unto him, to whom he had given the money, that he might know how much every man had gained by trading. Then came the first, saying, Lord, thy pound hath gained ten pounds. And he said unto him, Well, thou good servant: because thou hast been faithful in a very little, have thou authority over ten cities. And the second came, saying, Lord, thy pound hath gained five pounds. And he said likewise to him, Be

thou also over five cities. And another came, saying, Lord, behold, here is thy pound, which I have kept laid up in a napkin: For I feared thee, because thou art an austere man: thou takest up that thou layest not down, and reapest that thou didst not sow. And he saith unto him, Out of thine own mouth will I judge thee, thou wicked servant. Thou knewest that I was an austere man, taking up that I laid not down, and reaping that I did not sow: Wherefore then gavest not thou my money into the bank, that at my coming I might have required mine own with usury? And he said unto them that stood by, Take from him the pound, and give it to him that hath ten pounds. (And they said unto him, Lord, he hath ten pounds.) For I say unto you, That unto every one which hath shall be given; and from him that hath not, even that he hath shall be taken away from him. But those mine enemies, which would not that I should reign over them, bring hither, and slay them before me. (Luke 19:11-27)

Note that Jesus commended the servant who took that with which he had been entrusted by his master and used it wisely for the profit of the nobleman. In this and similar parables there is a strong indication that for those who have been faithful over a few things, "I will make thee ruler over many things: enter thou into the joy of thy lord" (Matt. 25:21). Responsibility without any of its earthly objectionable features will be a benediction of the rewards of heaven.

Rewards of possession or adornment are also mentioned in the Bible. For example, at least five different crowns are mentioned for various achievements. The first of these is addressed in 1 Corinthians 9:24-25:

Know ye not that they which run in a race run all, but one receiveth the prize? So run, that ye may obtain.

> And every man that striveth for the mastery is temperate in all things. Now they do it to obtain a corruptible crown; but we an incorruptible.

The crown mentioned here is not the diadem or kingly crown, but the *stephanos* or victor's wreath. Sometimes made of actual vines and leaves beautifully handwoven and at times formed of gold or silver to appear as a wreath or a garland, this crown was bestowed upon those who were victorious in the competitions of the day.

In this case, an incorruptible crown is the reward of those who strive for mastery in all things. Two words demand explanation. "Strive" (*agonizomenos*) gives us the English word *agonize*. It depicts maximum effort in the area of mastery (*egkrateuetai*) or the exercising of self-control. The practice of the world is to satisfy the lusts and cravings of the body. The practice of the believer who wishes to receive as a part of his reward the incorruptible victor's crown is to agonize for self-control.

The second crown mentioned is the crown of rejoicing to which Paul alluded in 1 Thessalonians 2:19: "For what is our hope, or joy, or crown of rejoicing? Are not even ye in the presence of our Lord Jesus Christ at his coming?" If one should object that this verse has no reference to a literal heavenly crown at all but rather to the fact that Paul's Thessalonian converts were like a crown of rejoicing to him, the point may be enthusiastically conceded. In fact that is the whole point and may even provide an index to the whole subject of "crowns" as "rewards." Every time we come across someone who is present in heaven in part as a result of our witness, it will be an experience crowned with rejoicing. So to the soul-winner goes the crown of rejoicing.

A crown of righteousness is the inheritance of all of those who love the day of Christ's return: "Henceforth there is laid up for me a crown of righteousness, which the Lord, the righteous judge, shall give me at that day: and not to me only, but unto all them also that love his appearing" (2 Tim. 4:8).

But do all not cherish the promise of the return of Christ? Sadly, the answer must be negative. Lack of understanding of the life of heaven and insensitivity to the will and purpose of God often cause even believers to cherish the present world order more than the kingdom of heaven. But for those who eagerly await His return, a crown of righteousness is waiting.

Throughout church history, many saints and martyrs of Christ have suffered incredible and inhuman testing. And all of God's people are tested and tempted in some fashion. James, the half brother of our Lord, advised the reader that these difficulties are not without reward and recognition: "Blessed is the man that endureth temptation: for when he is tried, he shall receive the crown of life, which the Lord hath promised to them that love him" (James 1:12).

This crown of life promised by Jesus, especially to those victimized by trials for Christ's sake, is also mentioned by John in the letter to the suffering congregation in Smyrna. Some would be cast into prison. But there should be no fear of suffering, since "I will give thee a crown of life" (Rev. 2:10).

> The elders which are among you I exhort, who am also an elder, and a witness of the sufferings of Christ, and also a partaker of the glory that shall be revealed: Feed the flock of God which is among you, taking the over- sight thereof, not by constraint, but willingly; not for filthy lucre, but of a ready mind; neither as being lords over God's heritage, but being ensamples to the flock. And when the chief Shepherd shall appear, ye shall receive a crown of glory that fadeth not away. (1 Pet. 5:1-4)

Shepherding is no simple task. It is often thankless, fre- quently tedious, and always unrelenting. But there is no greater calling. And when the chief Shepherd appears, these "undershepherds" will receive crowns of glory.

In chapter 4 of the Apocalypse, John observed twenty-four elders sitting on thrones located around the central throne of God. These elders (identified in chapter 5) have on their head the *stephanos* or victor's crown. When the cherubim begin to shout about the thrice holy nature of God, the twenty-four elders fall prostrate before the throne of the Lamb and cast their crowns before God. They recognize that even our "rewards" are actually little credit to us. They are rather additional evidence of the abounding grace of God toward sinners. He has saved us and then rewarded us abundantly. "O the depth of the riches both of the wisdom and knowledge of God! how unsearchable are his judgments and his ways past finding out!" (Rom. 11:33).

CHAPTER 13

Heaven and Hope

As if lightning had struck three times in one place, the Jews of Jerusalem were rocked in 606 B.C., 598 B.C., and 586 B.C. by the marching armies of Nebuchadnezzar of Babylon. Reduced to a vassal of Babylon in 606, Israel watched helplessly as a number of its most gifted young men, such as Daniel, Hananiah, Azariah, and Mishael, were deported. More, including Ezekiel, were transferred in 598. In 586, the city of Jerusalem was razed to the ground, followed by a massive deportation, leaving only the poor of the land and Jeremiah. These soon fled in fear to Egypt.

Devastated, the captives found themselves living in a refugee city on the banks of a man-made river, the Chebar, between the Tigris and Euphrates. There by the rivers of Babylon they sat and wept. Their captors required them to sing a song of Zion. Hanging their harps on the willows, the grieving homeless inquired as to how they could even sing the Lord's song in a strange land (Psalm 137). This dejection and defeat was the consequence of the sin of Israel, as the people clearly understood.

One day Ezekiel received a startling vision. Taken to a valley that had been the scene of a cataclysmic battle, the prophet saw the evidence of a terrible defeat of Israel. Birds of carrion and the weathering of the elements had done their work, scattering the skeletal remains of each former soldier. Ezekiel was asked if the bones could live again. On the one hand, the prophet knew that the answer was negative, but he did remember that it was God with whom he spoke. Wisely he replied, "Lord God, thou knowest" (Ezek. 37:3).

Now Ezekiel was instructed to preach first to the bones and then to the wind. The result was that the skeletons sorted themselves out, grew flesh, breathed, and stood as a very great army. Ezekiel did not need to seek an explanation for the vision. God said, "Son of man, these bones are the whole house of Israel: behold, they say, Our bones are dried and our hope is lost . . ." (Ezek. 37:11). Those last four words represented the conviction of every Jew in Babylon—"our hope is lost." Few greater tragedies overwhelm anyone than to lose hope. When a patient suffering severe illness loses hope, often he dies, regardless of the effectiveness of medication.

In Ephesians 2:11-12, Paul describes what it means for a man to be lost. Among other tragic conditions, the lost man is described as "having no hope" (Eph. 2:12). By contrast, Christ gives to the believer three abiding virtues that, according to the same apostle, endure when all else flickers and fails. In 1 Corinthians 13:13, Paul says, "And now abideth faith, hope, and charity, these three, and the greatest of these is charity." Probably no one would be surprised at the inclusion of faith and love in such a list, but to include hope suggests a role for hope in the revealed faith of God that few have contemplated.

Ezekiel's vision of the valley of dry bones was given to restore hope to the people of God in Babylon. They had incorrectly concluded that their hope was lost. Actually their best days lay ahead, and God, through Ezekiel's vision, called them to a beneficial hope for the future. And the theme of hope, whose strains are somewhat muted in the Old Testament, burst into a veritable crescendo of praise in the New Testament. But what is hope, and what are its appropriate objects? If hope is included with faith and love as critical virtues of the Lord's people, these questions are germane for life both here and hereafter.

The Nature of Biblical Hope

The concept of hope is employed in quite different ways in human speech. Someone may say, "I hope to inherit five million dollars." By this he may have in mind a certain prosperous uncle, advanced in age, but especially fond of him as nephew and heir. Or the statement may mean nothing more than "I wish I were wealthy and did not have to work to secure wealth." In other words "hope" is an idea that can be invoked with varying degrees of certainty. Sometimes it means nothing more than a distant, unlikely development for which one wishes but knows that it is not likely to develop. Or hope may refer to something that is absolutely certain though as yet unrealized. The certainty attached to that hope emerges from the trustworthiness of the one who has stirred the hope through promise. This latter sense is the way in which hope is inevitably presented in the Bible. In a sense, hope could be said to be the eschatalogical shading of faith.

Faith is the act of trust or commitment based on the mighty acts of God in history culminating in the birth, death, and resurrection of Jesus. We are told that if we place our faith in Jesus and His sacrifice, we will be saved. And this is precisely what happens when that faith is exercised. We experience forgiveness. We enjoy the new birth with its attitude-changing renovation of life. The consummation of salvation is yet in the future. The glorification of the body and the transfer to heaven are future and hence not yet realized. By faith we anticipate that this too will be a reality because of the faithfulness of Him who promised. This faith in a certain future is what is intended by hope in a biblical context.

One of the clearest statements of the nature of hope is provided by Paul in Romans 8:24-25: "For we are saved by hope: but hope that is seen is not hope: for what a man seeth, why doth he yet hope for? But if we hope for that we see not, then do we with patience wait for it." Again, as hope is defined as the unseen dimension of faith that has its fulfillment yet in the future, then this text stating that we are even "saved by hope" is perfectly explicable.

There is a contrast between this hope and hope that will disappoint. One of the greatest ethical chapters in the Bible is found in Job's testimony in chapter 31 of that book. He concludes that he would be worthy of certain judgment, "If I have made gold my hope, or have said to fine gold, Thou art my confidence" (Job 31:24). Hope in such material possessions not only will disappoint but also will be condemned. By contrast, Isaiah knows of a hope that is certain: "But they that wait upon the Lord shall renew their strength; they shall mount up with wings as eagles; they shall run, and not be weary; and they shall walk, and not faint" (Isa. 40:31).

This promise is echoed by the Psalmist who notes that "the eye of the Lord is upon them that fear him, upon them that hope in his mercy" (Ps. 33:18). God's mercy never fails; so hope in His mercy is a certainty, all aspects of which have not as yet come to fruition. But the Psalmist has seen enough so that he can exhort his own soul, saying, "Why art thou cast down, O my soul? And why art thou disquieted within me? hope in God: for I shall yet praise him, who is the health of my countenance, and my God" (Ps. 43:5).

Hope and the Resurrection
One topic with which hope is continually associated in the New Testament is the resurrection of the body. When Paul was hailed before the Sanhedrin and asked to address Israel's ruling

religious body, he astonished them by exploiting an old debate between the Pharisees and the Sadducees. Identifying himself as a Pharisee, he said, "Of the hope and resurrection of the dead I am called in question" (Acts 23:6). Again the nature of biblical hope as a certain but not yet realized event can be observed since Paul and the Pharisees were perfectly confident that the resurrection would take place.

Paul rehearsed a similar theme in his great dissertation on the resurrection of Jesus and ultimately of all believers recorded in 1 Corinthians 15. In the midst of this apology, Paul said, "If in this life only we have hope in Christ, we are of all men most miserable" (1 Cor. 15:19). Here Paul simply points to the futility of hope in temporal and material entities. If these constitute the only hope of a man, then he is miserable. But if there is a resurrection of the dead and if that resurrection is to a life that surpasses this one in opportunity and glory, then there is abundant reason for joy and happiness. The hope that the believer has is a "living hope," which has been irrevocably ignited in his heart "by the resurrection of Jesus Christ from the dead" (1 Pet. 1:3).

A practical benefit of this hope is the response of the believer in the face of the death of a loved one. In 1 Thessalonians 4:13, Paul encouraged: "But I would not have you to be ignorant, brethren, concerning them which are asleep, that ye sorrow not, even as others which have no hope."

It is interesting that Paul did not suggest that there be no sorrow at all. Humans often weep and experience a measure of sorrow when someone dear departs for a period of separation that is of only limited duration. Death for a believer is just that—a limited and, on the time-scale of eternity, brief dislocation. Thus for the unbeliever who has no hope, no faith-certainty, death is crushing, exceedingly sorrowful. The believer sorrows some over the momentary separation, but he does not sorrow as those who have no hope.

The Hope of Christ's Return

A cursory analysis of today's world will not inspire confidence. Confrontations, terrorism, and war abound in third-world countries and advanced civilizations alike. The whole of civilization seems to teeter perilously close to the edge of economic disaster. For all of the advances of medical technology, certain kinds of cancer are increasing, and the threat of AIDS and associated maladies complicate medical insurance unbelievably. World hunger continues to be the plight of millions, and the poisoning of the environment is a continuing concern. Can there be any hope in a dilemma like this?

In Titus 2:11-15, there occurs a passage of paramount hope and gracious instruction:

> For the grace of God that bringeth salvation hath appeared to all men. Teaching us that denying ungodliness and worldly lusts, we should live soberly, righteously, and godly, in this present world; Looking for that blessed hope, and the glorious appearing of the great God and our Savior Jesus Christ; who gave himself for us, that he might redeem us from all iniquity, and purify unto himself a peculiar people, zealous of good works. These things speak, and exhort, and rebuke with all authority. Let no man despise thee.

Living soberly, righteously, and godly in this present age is possible only if one can live expectantly. Discouragement and disillusionment are dispelled among those who know that there is a sure hope. That blessed hope is the appearing of the great God and Savior Jesus Christ. And the hope in His appearing is based solidly on the fact that He appeared initially exactly as promised by Old Testament prophets. The redemption that He purchased by giving himself for us convinces us that His coming appearance will be greater glory still. Thus Paul could say in Colossians 1:27, "Christ in you the hope of glory." That is to say the indwelling Christ is the certain hope that there will be glory and heaven to come.

In fact, one aspect of the hope of the coming of Christ that ought to be extraordinarily precious to Christians is the hope of being made totally righteous in that day. Even when we make our best and noblest efforts, they are tinged with the guilt of our own selfishness. And, of course, there are those all-too-frequent times when we sin gravely. The things we wish we would do we fail to do, while the things we wish to avoid, we still do (Rom. 7:19). No wonder Paul took comfort in Galatians 5:5 by noting that "we through the spirit wait for the hope of righteousness by faith." When Jesus comes, we shall be made finally righteous—free from all sin!

The Effects of Hope

In addition to the mitigations of sorrow in moments of death, there are other consequences of the hope cherished by Christians. Simon Peter alluded to one such benefit in his Pentecostal sermon recorded in Acts 2. Peter cited Psalm 16:8-11 and spoke of Jesus as the fulfillment of a prophecy uttered by King David more than one thousand years before Christ:

> For David speaketh concerning him, I foresaw the Lord always before my face; for he is on my right hand, that I should not be moved: therefore did my heart rejoice, and my tongue was glad; moreover also my flesh shall rest in hope. (Acts 2:25-26)

Note the phrase "rest in hope." Sorrows at death constitute only a small portion of the disappointments of life. Uncertainty as to what will happen in the future and fear of the unknown are features of life that are most disquieting. But the redeemed have learned to "rest in hope." This is hope born out of a perfect confidence in the providence of God. As Jesus put it, "If ye then, being evil, know how to give good gifts unto your children, how much more shall your Father which is in heaven give good things to them that ask him?" (Matt. 7:11). We rest in perfect hope of the intervening providence of God.

Another benefit of eschatalogical hope is that of motivation to purity of life.

> Behold, what manner of love the Father hath bestowed upon us, that we should be called the sons of God: therefore the world knoweth us not, because it knew him not. Beloved, now are we the sons of God, and it doth not yet appear what we shall be: but we know that, when he shall appear, we shall be like him; for we shall see him as he is. And every man that hath this hope in him purifieth himself, even as he is pure. (1 John 3:1-3)

The presence of hope, knowing that any day, any hour, the trumpet of God might be heard, Christ might appear, and our heavenly home might become our permanent and eternal residence ought to provide ultimate motivation for purity and holiness of life. A person may theologize or preach about the return of the Lord and heaven to come and still live a reprobate existence. But actually to hope in the appearing of Christ is to live in eager expectation of that event. And to live expectantly is to purify oneself.

Finally, to have this hope is to become an apologist and witness for Jesus. "But sanctify the Lord God in your hearts: and be ready always to give an answer to every man that asketh you a reason of the hope that is in you with meekness and fear" (1 Pet. 3:15).

Peter suggested that the hope of believers will spawn questions among unbelievers as to the nature and reason of that hope. People reeling under the blows of a hostile and insensitive world tend to forfeit hope rather quickly. Crossing paths with spiritual optimists who have a living hope is almost certain to engender questions relating to the reasons for such hope. Peter challenged all born-again believers to be ready to give an answer (*apologia,* Greek) to everyone who asks a reason for that hope. The apologist is then able to direct the inquirer to the hope of forgiveness, the hope of cleansing, the hope of Christ's return, the hope of resurrection and triumph over death, and the hope of heaven.

Thus, one may conclude that the hope of Christ's return and of the kind of heaven presented on the pages of Scripture constitute a unique hope unmatched in any other faith. Further, in a faceless world of discouraging news and widespread cynicism, the hope of heaven is one of the most therapeutic doctrines for the sick soul of humanity.

CONCLUSION

By faith Abraham, when he was called to go out into a place which he should after receive for an inheritance, obeyed; and he went out, not knowing whither he went. By faith he sojourned in the land of promise, as in a strange country, dwelling in tabernacles with Isaac and Jacob, the heirs with him of the same promise. For he looked for a city which hath foundations, whose builder and maker is God. (Heb. 11:8-10)

Somehow Abraham, beginning a long, tedious journey in the troubled Ur of the Chaldees, realized that the city for which he longed would not be of this world. Ur of Abraham's day was a large and beautiful desert city. Along the way of his sojourn, he passed through other cities of grand design and imperial embellishment. They were all incomplete and imperfect, the habitations of fallen men. Even in Canaan, the Promised Land, there were problems, and Abraham himself was sometimes one of those problems. Surely there must be a better place.

Therefore, by faith Abraham searched for a city "whose builder and maker is God." In the story Jesus told in Luke 16, Lazarus died and was ferried by the angels "into Abraham's bosom." Not only did Abraham and Lazarus discover the city which has permanent foundations and whose builder and maker is God, but also every redeemed person will discover that ultimate abode. Our descriptions of heaven, including many details, may suffer from paucity of information and limitation of human vocabulary, but enough is present in the Scriptures to convince us of the wonder and desirability of that place.

We join John at the conclusion of his arresting description of the heavenly city in Revelation 21 and 22 with a final invitation to all readers to join us in that glorious citadel.

"And the Spirit and the bride say, Come. And let him that heareth say, Come. And let him that is athirst come. And whosoever will, let him take the water of life freely" (Rev. 22:17).

PART THREE
Great Hymns and Poems about Heaven

Ring the Bells of Heaven

Ring the bells of heaven! there is joy today
For a soul returning from the wild!
See! the Father meets him out upon the way,
Welcoming His weary, wand'ring child.

Ring the bells of heaven! there is joy today,
For the wand'rer now is reconciled;
Yes, a soul is rescued from his sinful way,
And is born anew a ransomed child.

Ring the bells of heaven! spread the feast today!
Angels, swell the glad triumphant strain!
Tell the joyful tidings, bear it far away!
For a precious soul is born again.

Glory! glory! how the angels sing;
Glory! glory! how the loud harps ring!
'Tis the ransomed army, like a mighty sea,
Pealing forth the anthem of the free!

William O. Cushing, 1823–1902 George F. Root, 1820–1895

"Likewise, I say unto you, there is joy in the presence of the angels of God over one sinner that repenteth" (Luke 15:10).Though this musical cadence was written by Dr. Root for a secular song, Cushing could not escape the flowing, sweet melody. One day when he heard about the return of a sinner to the fold, it seemed to his own soul that the very bells of heaven were ringing, and these words easily fit into this waiting melody.

Beyond the Sunset

Beyond the sunset, O blissful morning,
When with our Savior heav'n is begun.
Earth's toiling ended, O glorious dawning;
Beyond the sunset, when day is done.

Beyond the sunset no clouds will gather,
No storms will threaten, no fears annoy;
O day of gladness, O day unending,
Beyond the sunset, eternal joy!

Beyond the sunset a hand will guide me
To God, the Father, whom I adore;
His glorious presence, His words of welcome,
Will be my portion on that fair shore.

Beyond the sunset, O glad reunion,
With our dear loved ones who've gone before;
In that fair homeland we'll know no parting,
Beyond the sunset for evermore!

Virgil P. Brock   Blanche Kerr Brock

The Promised Land

On Jordan's rugged banks I stand,
  And cast a wishful eye
To Canaan's fair and happy land,
  Where my possessions lie.

O the transporting, rapt'rous scene
  That rises to my sight!
Sweet fields array'd in living green,
  And rivers of delight!

There generous fruits, that never fail,
  On trees immortal grow:
There rocks, and hills, and brooks, and vales,
  With milk and honey flow.

All o'er those wide extended plains
  Shines one eternal day!
There God the Sun for ever reigns,
  And scatters night away.

No chilling winds; or pois'nous breath,
  Can reach that healthful shore:
Sickness and sorrow, pain and death,
  Are felt and fear'd no more.

When shall I reach that happy place,
  And be for ever blest?
When shall I see my Father's face,
  And in his bosom rest?

Fill'd with delight, my raptur'd soul
  Can here no longer stay
Tho' Jordan's waves around me roll,
  Fearless I'd launch away.

Dr. Samuel Stennett, 1787

Heaven

On wings of faith, mount up, my soul; and rise;
View thine inheritance beyond the skies;
Nor heart can think; nor mortal tongue can tell,
What endless pleasures in those mansions dwell:

Chorus
Here our Redeemer lives, all bright, and glorious,
O'er sin, and death, and hell, he reigns victorious.

No gnawing grief, no sad heart-rending pain,
In that blest country can admission gain;
No sorrow there, no soul tormenting fear,
For God's own hand shall wipe the falling tear.

(Chorus)
Before the throne a crystal river glides,
Immortal verdure decks its cheerful sides:
Here the fair tree of life majestic rears
Its blooming head, and sovereign virtue bears:

(Chorus)
No rising sun his needless beams displays;
No sickly moon emits her feeble rays;
The Godhead here celestial glory sheds,
Th' exalted Lamb eternal radiance spreads:

(Chorus)
One distant glimpse my eager passion fires!
Jesus! to thee my longing soul aspires!
When shall I at thy heavenly home arrive,—
When leave this earth; and when begin to live?

Chorus
For here my Savior is all bright and glorious;
O'er sin, and death, and hell he reigns victorious.

J. Staphan

The Grapes of Canaan or Heaven Anticipated

Too long, alas! I vainly sought
  For happiness below,
But earthly joys, though dearly bought,
  No solid good bestow.

At length, thro' sov'reign Grace, I found
  The good and promis'd land,
Where milk and honey flow around;
  And grapes in clusters stand.

As I have tasted of the grapes,
  I sometimes long to go
Where my dear Lord his vineyard keeps,
  And all the clusters grow.

And can I long, and taste the fruit,
  And Canaan be deny'd?
Those who taste the fruits of grace
  Must all be glorify'd.

This hymn is an expression of heaven anticipated.

Realms of Glory

Look, ye saints, the sight is glorious:
  See the man of sorrows now;
From the fight returned victorious,
  Ev'ry knee to Him shall bow;
Crown Him! Crown Him!
Crowns become the victor's brow.

Sinners in derision crowned Him,
  Mocking thus the Saviour's claim;
Saints and angels crowd around Him,
  Own His title, Praise His name:
Crown Him! Crown Him!
Spread abroad the victor's fame!

Hark! Those bursts of acclamation! Hark!
Those loud triumphant chords!
Jesus takes the highest station;
  O What joy the sight affords!
Crown Him! Crown Him!
King of Kings, and Lord of Lords.

Thomas Kelly, 1809

"We see Jesus . . . crowned with glory and honor" (Heb.
2:9). Thomas Kelly, recognized as one of nineteenth-century
Ireland's finest evangelical preachers as well as one of her
most distinguished and spiritual poets, composed almost
eight hundred hymn texts. This is recognized as one of the
finest Ascension Day hymns.

There is a land of pure delight,
  Where saints immortal reign:
Infinite day excludes the night,
  And pleasures banish pain.

There everlasting spring abides,
  And never-withering flowers;
Death, like a narrow sea, divides
  This heavenly land from ours.

Sweet fields, beyond the swelling flood,
  Stand dressed in living green;
So to the Jews old Canaan stood,
  While Jordan rolled between.

But timorous mortals start and shrink
  To cross this narrow sea,
And linger, shivering on the brink,
  And fear to launch away.

Oh, could we make our doubts remove,
  These gloomy doubts that rise,
And see the Canaan that we love,
  With unbeclouded eyes:—

Could we but climb where Moses stood,
  And view the landscape o'er, —
Not Jordan's stream, nor death's cold flood,
  Should fright us from the shore.

Isaac Watts

Arise, my soul, fly up, and run
  Through every heavenly street;
And say there's nought below the sun
  That's worthy of thy feet.

There, on a high, majestic throne,
  Th' Almighty Father reigns,
And sheds His glorious goodness down
  On all the blissful plains.

Bright, like a sun, the Savior sits,
  And spreads eternal noon;
No evenings there, nor gloomy nights,
  To want the feeble moon.

Amidst those ever-shining skies
  Behold the sacred Dove;
While banished sin and sorrow flies
  From all the realms of love.

But O, what beams of heavenly grace
  Transport them all the while!
Then thousand smiles from Jesus' face,
  And love in every smile!

Jesus, and when shall that dear day,
  That joyful hour appear,
When I shall leave this house of clay,
  To dwell among them there?

Isaac Watts

Joyful Work for You

Earth has engrossed my love too long!
  'Tis time I lift mine eyes
Upward, dear Father, to Thy throne,
  And to my native skies.

There the blessed Man, my Savior sits;
  The God! how bright he shines!
And scatters infinite delights
  On all the happy minds.

Seraphs, with elevated strains,
  Circle the throne around;
And move and charm the starry plains,
  With an immortal sound.

Jesus, the Lord, their harps employs;
  Jesus my love they sing!
Jesus, the life of all our joys,
  Sounds sweet from every string.

Now let me mount and join their song,
  And be an angel, too;
My heart, my hand, my ear, my tongue,—
  Here's joyful work for you.

I would begin the music here,
  And so my soul should rise;
O for some heavenly notes to bear
  My passions to the skies!

There ye that love my Savior sit,
  There I would fain have place,
Among your thrones, or at your feet,
  So I might see His face.

Issac Watts

Enter to Thy Rest

There is a glorious world of light,
  Above the starry sky,
Where saints departed, clothed in white,
  Adore the Lord most high.

And hark! amid the sacred songs
  Those heavenly voices raise,
Ten thousand thousand infant tongues
  Unite in perfect praise.

Those are the hymns that we shall know,
  If Jesus we obey:
That is the place where we will go,
  If found in wisdom's way.

Soon will our earthly race be run,
  Our mortal frame decay;
Parents and children, one by one,
  Must die and pass away.

Great God, impress the serious thought,
  This day, on every breast,
That both the teachers and the taught
  May enter to Thy rest.

Jane Taylor

O My Sweet Home

O happy harbor of God's saints!
O sweet and pleasant soil!
In thee no sorrow can be found,
Nor grief, nor care, nor toil.

No dimly cloud o'ershadows thee,
Nor gloom, nor darksome night;
But every soul shines as the sun,
For God himself gives light.

Thy walls are made of precious stone,
Thy bulwarks diamond-square,
Thy gates are all of orient pearl—
O God! if I were there!

O my sweet home, Jerusalem!
Thy joys when shall I see?—
The King that sitteth on thy throne
In His felicity?

Thy gardens and thy goodly walks
Continually are green,
Where grow such sweet and pleasant flowers
As no where else are seen.

Right thro' thy streets with pleasing sound
The flood of life doth flow;
And on the banks, on either side,
The trees of life do grow.

Those trees each month yield ripened fruit;
For evermore they spring,
And all the nations of the earth
To thee their honors bring.

O mother dear, Jerusalem!
When shall I come to thee?

When shall my sorrows have an end?
  Thy joys when shall I see?

Francis Quarles

O That Will Be Glory

When all my labors and trials are o'er
And I am safe on that beautiful shore,
Just to be near the dear Lord I adore
Will through the ages be glory for me.

Chorus
O that will be glory for me,
Glory for me, glory for me;
When by His grace I shall look on His face,
That will be glory, be glory for me!

When, by the gift of His infinite grace,
I am accorded in heaven a place,
Just to be there and to look on his face
Will through the ages be glory for me.

(Chorus)
Friends will be there I have loved long ago,
Joy like a river around me will flow;
Yet, just a smile from my Savior, I know.
Will through the ages be glory for me.
(Chorus)

Charles H. Gabriel

"And God shall wipe away all tears from their eyes; and there shall be no more death, neither sorrow, nor crying, neither shall there be any more pain: for the former things are passed away" (Rev. 21:4). One of twentieth-century America's most influential and prolific gospel songwriters, Charles

Gabriel usually wrote both texts and music for his songs. This text was inspired by the life of Gabriel's good friend, Ed Card, a radiant believer who always seemed to be bubbling over with the joy of the Lord. It was not uncommon for him to explode during a prayer or sermon with the expression, "Glory!" He always ended his own prayers with a reference to heaven and the phrase, "And that will be glory for me." It has been reported that Card had the pleasure of singing this hymn just before his own home going, knowing that his own life had inspired its message.

My Father Is Rich in Houses and Lands

My Father is rich in houses and lands,
He holdeth the wealth of the world in His hands!
Of rubies and diamonds, of silver and gold,
His coffers are full, He has riches untold.

My Father's own Son, the Savior of men,
Once wandered on earth as the poorest of them;
But now He is reigning forever on high,
And will give me a home in heav'n by and by.

I once was an outcast stranger on earth,
A sinner by choice, and an alien by birth;
But I've been adopted, my name's written down
An heir to a mansion, a robe, and a crown.

A tent or a cottage, why should I care?
They're building a palace for me over there;
Though exiled from home, yet still I may sing:
All glory to God, I'm a child of the King.

I'm a child of the King, a child of the King:
With Jesus my Savior, I'm a child of the King.

Harriett E. Buell

Jerusalem, My Happy Home

Jerusalem, my happy home
When shall I come to thee?
When shall my sorrows have an end?
Thy joys when shall I see?

O happy harbor of the saints,
O sweet and pleasant soil!
In thee, no sorrow may be found,
No grief, no care, no toil.

Thy saints are crowned with glory great;
They see God face to face;
They triumph still, they still rejoice:
Most happy is their case.

There David stands with harp in hand
As master of the choir:
Ten thousand times that man were blest
That might this music hear.

Jerusalem, my happy home,
Would God I were in thee!
Would God my woes were at an end,
Thy joys that I might see!

Based on anonymous sixteenth-century hymn

I'm Just a Poor, Wayfaring Stranger

I'm just a poor wayfaring stranger,
A trav'ling through this world of woe;
But there's no sickness, no toil or danger,
In that bright world to which I go.
I'm going there to see my mother,
I'm going there, no more to roam,

I'm just a going over Jordan,
I'm just a going over home.

American folk hymn

Love Divine, So Great and Wondrous

Love divine, so great and wondrous,
Deep and mighty, pure, sublime;
Coming from the heart of Jesus—
Just the same thro' tests of time.

Like a dove when hunted, frightened,
As a wounded fawn was I,
Broken hearted, yet He healed me—
He will heed the sinner's cry.

Love divine, so great and wondrous—
All my sins He then forgave,
I will sing His praise forever,
For his blood, his pow'r to save.

He the pearly gates will open,
So that I may enter in;
For He purchased my redemption,
And forgave me all my sin.

Frederick A. Blom

I Belong to the King

I belong to the King, I'm a child of His love,
I shall dwell in His palace so fair;
For He tells of its bliss in yon heaven above,
And His children its splendors shall share.

I belong to the King, and He loves me, I know,
For His mercy and kindness, so free,

184

Are unceasingly mine wheresoever I go,
And my refuge unfailing is He.

I belong to the King, and His promise is sure,
That we all shall be gathered at last
In His kingdom above, by life's waters so pure,
When this life with its trials is past.

I belong to the King, I'm a child of His love,
And He never forsaketh His own;
He will call me some day to His palace above,
I shall dwell by His glorified throne.

Ida R. Smith

Come, Come, Ye Saints

Come, come, ye saints, no toil nor labor fear,
But with joy wend your way;
Though hard to you life's journey may appear,
Grace shall be as your day.
God's hand of love shall be your guide,
And all your need He will provide;
His pow'r shall every foe dispel,
All is well, All is well!

What though the path you tread be rough and steep?
Have no fear, He is near!
His mighty arm unto the end will keep;
Soon His call you shall hear.
Then follow on, fresh courage take,
For God His own will ne'er forsake,
Till in His presence they shall dwell!
All is well, All is well!

God hath prepared a glorious Home above
Round His throne, for His own,

Where they may rest forever in His love,
Toil and tears all unknown.
There they shall sing eternal praise
To Him who saved them by his grace.
Through heaven's courts the song shall swell,
All is well, All is well!

With longing hearts we wait the promised day
When the trump we shall hear,
That summons us from earthly cares away,
At His side to appear!
But until then we'll labor on
In patience till our course is run,
Although the hour we may not tell,
All is well, All is well!

Avis B. Christiansen

Face to Face with Christ My Savior

Face to face with Christ my Savior,
Face to face—what will it be?
When with rapture I behold Him,
Jesus Christ who died for me?

Only faintly now I see Him,
With the darkling veil between;
But a blessed day is coming,
When his glory shall be seen.

What rejoicing in His presence,
When are banished grief and pain,
When the crooked ways are straightened
And the dark things shall be plain.

Face to face—O blissful moment!
Face to face to see and know;

Face to face with my Redeemer,
Jesus Christ who loves me so!

Face to face I shall behold Him,
Far beyond the starry sky;
Face to face, in all His glory,
I shall see him by and by!

Carrie E. Breck

Shall We Gather at the River?

Shall we gather at the river,
Where bright angel feet have trod,
With its crystal tide forever
Flowing by the throne of God?

On the bosom of the river,
Where the Savior-King we own,
We shall meet and sorrow never
'Neath the glory of the throne.

Ere we reach the shining river,
Lay we ev'ry burden down;
Grace our spirits will deliver
And provide a robe and crown.

Soon we'll reach the shining river,
Soon our pilgrimage will cease;
Soon our happy hearts will quiver
With the melody of peace.

Yes, we'll gather at the river,
The beautiful, the beautiful river,
Gather with the saints at the river
That flows by the throne of God.

Robert Lowry

Educator, orator, administrator, poet, musician, and
preacher, Robert Lowry was in the midst of a deadly
epidemic in New York City when he wrote this hymn.
He was inspired by the thought of a coming happy reunion
with those friends and parishioners who had crossed over
Jordan from death to life.

On Jordan's Stormy Banks

On Jordan's stormy banks I stand
And cast a wishful eye
To Canaan's fair and happy land,
Where my possessions lie.

All o'er those wide-extended plains
Shines one eternal day;
There God the Son forever reigns
And scatters night away.

No chilling winds nor pois'nous breath
Can reach that healthful shore;
Sickness and sorrow, pain and death
Are felt and feared no more.

When shall I reach that happy place
And be forever blest?
When shall I see my Father's face
And in His bosom rest?

I am bound for the promised land,
I am bound for the promised land;
O who will come and go with me?
I am bound for the promised land.

Samuel Stennett (1727–1795)

This beloved hymn was already a century old when sung by Confederate youth Sam Davis before his death by hanging. He had been offered freedom for cooperation in the capture of his elusive leader. Davis told the hangman, "Had I a thousand lives, I would lose them all here before I would betray a friend."

Finally Home

When engulfed by the terror of tempestuous sea,—
Unknown waves before you roll;
At the end of doubt and peril is eternity,—
Though fear and conflict seize your soul:

When surrounded by the blackness of the darkest night,
O how lonely death can be;
At the end of this long tunnel is a shining light,
For death is swallowed up in victory!

But just think of stepping on shore—
and finding it heaven!
Of touching a hand—
and finding it God's!
Of breathing new air and finding it celestial!
Of waking up in glory—
and finding it home!

Don Wyrtzen   L. E. Singer

The lyrics of this gospel song originally were the words of an anonymous poem entitled "The Homeland." Mrs. Ruth Hunt uncovered the poem and shared it with her pastor, Dr. Criswell, who quoted the poem in a tent revival meeting sometime between 1975 and 1978 in Gatlinburg, Tennessee.

His daughter Anne had accompanied him to this revival to present the messages in music each night. According to Anne, she was so impressed with the poem discovered by Ruth Hunt and shared by her father in that revival, that she asked Don Wyrtzen, who was her accompanist, if he would put the words to music. That he did, and Anne has claimed "Finally Home" as her song ever since. She sang it at a service in Boca Raton, Florida, where Pat Zondervan heard it. He liked it so much that he asked Don Wyrtzen to write more verses, and the words of the poem then became the chorus of the expanded song. Don and Anne together came up with the title "Finally Home."

When I Can Read My Title Clear

When I can read my title clear
To mansions in the skies,
I'll bid farewell to ev'ry fear
And wipe my weeping eyes.

Should earth against my soul engage,
And fiery darts be hurled,
Then I can smile at Satan's rage
And face a frowning world.

Let cares, like a wild deluge come,
And storms of sorrow fall!
May I but safely reach my home,
My God, my heav'n, my all.

There shall I bathe my weary soul
In seas of heav'nly rest,
And not a wave of trouble roll
Across my peaceful breast.

Isaac Watts

When We All Get to Heaven

Sing the wondrous love of Jesus,
Sing His mercy and His grace;
In the mansions bright and blessed
He'll prepare for us a place.

While we walk the pilgrim pathway
Clouds will overspread the sky;
But when trav'ling days are over
Not a shadow, not a sigh.

Let us then be true and faithful,
Trusting, serving ev'ry day;
Just one glimpse of Him in glory
Will the toils of life repay.

Onward to the prize before us!
Soon His beauty we'll behold;
Soon the pearly gates will open—
We shall tread the streets of gold.

When we all get to heaven,
What a day of rejoicing that will be!
When we all see Jesus,
We'll sing and shout the victory.

Eliza E. Hewitt

After

After the toil and the heat of the day,
After my troubles are past,
After the sorrows are taken away,
I shall see Jesus at last.

After the heartaches and sighing shall cease,
After the cold winter's blast,

After the conflict comes glorious peace—
I shall see Jesus at last.

After the shadows of evening shall fall,
After my anchor is cast,
After I list to my Savior's last call,
I shall see Jesus at last.

He will be waiting for me—
Jesus so kind and true;
On His beautiful throne,
He will welcome me home
After the day is through.

N. B. Vandall

My Savior First of All

When my life-work is ended and I cross the swelling tide,
When the bright and glorious morning I shall see,
I shall know my Redeemer when I reach the other side,
And His smile will be the first to welcome me.

O the soul-thrilling rapture when I view his blessed face
And the luster of His kindly beaming eye;
How my full heart will praise Him for the mercy,
    love and grace
That prepare for me a mansion in the sky.

O the dear ones in glory, how they beckon me to come,
And our parting at the river I recall;
To the sweet vales of Eden they will sing my welcome home—
But I long to meet my Savior first of all.

Through the gates to the city in a robe of spotless white,
He will lead me where no tears will ever fall;
In the glad song of ages I shall mingle with delight—
But I long to meet my Savior first of all.

I shall know Him, I shall know Him,
And redeemed by His side I shall stand,
I shall know Him, I shall know Him
By the print of the nails in His hand.

Fanny J. Crosby (1820–1915)   John R. Sweeney (1837–1899)

My Home, Sweet Home

Walking along life's road one day,
I heard a voice so sweetly say,
"A place up in heav'n I am building thee,
A beautiful, beautiful home."

Loved ones upon that shore I'll meet,
Casting their crowns at Jesus' feet;
I'll worship and praise Him forevermore
In my beautiful, beautiful home.

Life's day is short—I soon shall go
To be with him who loved me so;
I see in the distance that shining shore,
My beautiful, beautiful home.

Home, sweet home, home, sweet home—
Where I'll never roam!
I see the light of that city so bright—
My home, sweet home.

N. B. Vandall

Sweet By and By

There's a land that is fairer than day,
And by faith we can see it afar,
For the Father waits over the way
To prepare us a dwelling place there.

We shall sing on that beautiful shore
The melodious songs of the blest;
And our spirits shall sorrow no more—
Not a sigh for the blessing of rest.

To our bountiful Father above
We will offer our tribute of praise,
For the Glorious gift of His love
And the blessings that hallow our days.

In the sweet by and by,
We shall meet on that beautiful shore;
In the sweet by and by,
We shall meet on that beautiful shore.

Sanford F. Bennett, 1868

A nineteenth-century general practitioner of medicine, Dr. Sanford Bennett wrote verse as a hobby. His collaborator Joseph Webster once came into Bennett's office in a state of depression. When Bennett asked, "What's the trouble now," Webster replied, "Oh . . . everything will be all right by and by." That idle remark inspired this beautiful hymn which was written and sung within the hour.

When the Roll Is Called Up Yonder

When the trumpet of the Lord shall sound and time
  shall be no more,
And the morning breaks eternal, bright and fair—
When the saved of earth shall gather over on the other shore,
And the roll is called up yonder I'll be there!

On that bright and cloudless morning when the dead
  in Christ shall rise

And the glory of His resurrection share—
When His chosen ones shall gather to their home beyond the skies,
And the roll is called up yonder I'll be there!

Let us labor for the Master from the dawn till setting sun,
Let us talk of all His wondrous love and care;
Then when all of life is over and our work on earth is done,
And the roll is called up younder I'll be there!

When the roll is called up yonder,
When the roll is called up yonder,
When the roll is called up yonder—
When the roll is called up yonder I'll be there!

James M. Black, 1893

What a Gathering

On that bright and golden morning when the
  Son of Man shall come,
And the radiance of His glory we shall see,
When from ev'ry clime and nation He shall
  call His people home,
What a gath'ring of the ransomed that will be!

When the blest who sleep in Jesus at His bidding shall arise
From the silence of the grave and from the sea,
And with bodies all celestial they shall meet Him
  in the skies,
What a gath'ring and rejoicing there will be!

When our eyes behold the city with its many mansions bright
And its river, calm and restful, flowing free,
When the friends that death hath parted shall in bliss
  again unite,
What a gath'ring and a greeting there will be!

O the King is surely coming, and the time is drawing nigh
When the blessed day of promise we shall see;
Then the changing "in a moment, in the twinkling of an eye,"
And forever in His presence we shall be.

What a gath'ring, what a gath'ring,
What a gath'ring of the ransomed
In the summer land of love!
What a gath'ring, what a gath'ring
Of the ransomed in that happy home above!

Fanny J. Crosby

The Unclouded Day

O they tell me of a home far beyond the skies,
O they tell me of a home far away;
O they tell me of a home where no storm-clouds rise,
O they tell me of an unclouded day.

O they tell me of a home where my friends have gone,
O they tell me of a land far away,
Where the tree of life in eternal bloom
Sheds its fragrance thro' the unclouded day.

O they tell me of a King in His beauty there,
And they tell me that mine eyes shall behold
Where He sits on the throne that is whiter than snow,
In the city that is made of gold.

O they tell me that He smiles on His children there,
And His smile drives their sorrows all away;
And they tell me that no tears ever come again,
In that lovely land of unclouded day.

O the land of cloudless day,
O the land of an unclouded day;
O they tell me of a home where no storm-clouds rise,
O they tell me of an unclouded day.

Rev. J. K. Alwood

I Will Not Be a Stranger

I will not be a stranger when I get to that city,
I'm acquainted with folks over there;
There'll be friends there to greet me,
There'll be loved ones to meet me,
At the gates of that city foursquare.

I will not be a stranger when I get to that city,
I've a home on those streets paved with gold;
I will feel right at home there in that beautiful
    "Somewhere,"
With my loved ones whose mem'ries I hold.

I will not be a stranger when I get to that city,
There'll be no lonely days over there;
There'll be no stormy weather but a great get together,
On the streets of that city foursquare.

Through the years, through the tears, they have gone
    one by one,
But they'll wait at the gate, until my race is run;
I will not be a stranger when I get to that city,
I'm acquainted with folks over there.

James B. Singleton

How Beautiful Heaven Must Be

We read of a place that's called heaven,
It's made for the pure and the free;
These truths in God's Word He hath given,
How beautiful heaven must be.

In heaven no drooping nor pining,
No wishing for elsewhere to be;
God's light is forever there shining,
How beautiful heaven must be.

Pure waters of life there are flowing,
And all who will drink may be free;
Rare jewels of spendor are glowing.
How beautiful heaven must be.

The angels so sweetly are singing,
Up there by the beautiful sea;
Sweet chords from their gold harps are ringing.
How beautiful heaven must be.

How beautiful heaven must be,
Sweet home of the happy and free;
Fair haven of rest for the weary,
How beautiful heaven must be.

A. P. Bland

Where We'll Never Grow Old

I have heard of a land on the far away strand,
'Tis a beautiful home of the soul;
Built by Jesus on high, there we never shall die,
'Tis a land where we never grow old.

In that beautiful home where we'll nevermore roam,
We shall be in the sweet by and by;
Happy praise to the King through eternity sing,
'Tis a land where we never shall die.

When our work here is done and the life-crown is won,
And our troubles and trials are o'er;
All our sorrows will end and our voices will blend,
With the loved ones who've gone on before.

Never grow old, Never grow old,
In a land where we'll never grow old;
Never grow old, Never grow old,
In a land where we'll never grow old.

James C. Moore

Inspired by the singing of his godly father, James Moore wrote this hymn in his youth. When James's father preached his last sermon, from the pulpit he extracted a promise from his son that this great hymn, written by the younger Moore, would be sung when the Lord called him home.

Jerusalem the Golden

Jerusalem the golden,
With milk and honey blest,
Beneath thy contemplation
Sink heart and voice oppressed:
I know not, O I know not,
What joys await me there,
What radiancy of glory,
What bliss beyond compare!

They stand, those halls of Zion,
All jubilant with song,
And bright with many an angel,
And all the martyr throng;
The Prince is ever in them,
The daylight is serene,
The pastures of the blessed
Are decked in glorious sheen.

There is the throne of David;
And there, from care released,
The song of them that triumph,
The shout of them that feast;
And they, who with their Leader
Have conquered in the fight,
Forever and forever
Are clad in robes of white.

O sweet and blessed country,
The home of God's elect!
O sweet and blessed country
That eager hearts expect!
Jesus, in mercy bring us
To that dear land of rest;
Who art, with God the Father,
And Spirit, every blest.

Bernard of Cluny (12th century)

The Sands of Time Are Sinking

The sands of time are sinking
The dawn of heaven breaks;

The summer morn I've sighed for—
The fair, sweet morning awakes:
Dark, dark hath been the midnight,
But dayspring is at hand,
And glory, glory dwelleth
In Immanuel's land.

O Christ, He is the fountain,
The deep, sweet well of love!
The streams on earth I've tasted
More deep I'll drink above:
There to an ocean fulness
His mercy doth expand,
And glory, glory dwelleth
In Immanuel's land.

O I am my Beloved's,
And my Beloved's mine!
He brings a poor vile sinner
Into His "house of wine."
I stand upon His merit—
I know no other stand,
Not e'en where glory dwelleth
In Immanuel's land.

The Bride eyes not her garment
But her dear Bridegroom's face;
I will not gaze at glory
But on my King of grace.
Not at the crown He giveth
But on His pierced hand:
The Lamb is all the glory of Immanuel's land.

Anne Ross Cousin

We're Marching to Zion

Come, we that love the Lord,
And let our joys be known;
Join in a song with sweet accord,
Join in a song with sweet accord
And thus surround the throne,
And thus surround the throne.

Let those refuse to sing
Who never knew our God;
But children of the heav'nly King,
But children of the heav'nly King
May speak their joys abroad,
May speak their joys abroad.

The hill of Zion yields
A thousand sacred sweets
Before we reach the heav'nly fields,
Before we reach the heav'nly fields
Or walk the golden streets,
Or walk the golden streets.

Then let our songs abound
And ev'ry tear be dry;
We're marching through Immanuel's ground,
We're marching through Immanuel's ground
To fairer worlds on high,
To fairer worlds on high.

We're marching to Zion,
Beautiful, beautiful Zion;
We're marching upward to Zion,
The beautiful city of God.

Isaac Watts

Beulah Land

I've reached the land of corn and wine,
And all its riches freely mine;
Here shines undimmed one blissful day,
For all my night has passed away.

My Savior comes and walks with me,
And sweet communion here have we;
He gently leads me by His hand,
For this is heaven's borderland.

A sweet perfume upon the breeze
Is borne from ever vernal trees
And flow'rs that never fading grow,
Where streams of life forever flow.

The zephyrs seem to float to me
Sweet sounds of heaven's melody,
As angels with the white-robed throng
Join in the sweet Redemption song.

O Beulah Land, sweet Beulah Land!
As on thy highest mount I stand,
I look away across the sea,
Where mansions are prepared for me,
And view the shining glory-shore—
My heav'n, my home forevermore!

Edgar Page Stites

Meet Me There

On the happy, golden shore
Where the faithful part no more,
When the storms of life are o'er,
Meet me there;

Where the night dissolves away
Into pure and perfect day,
I am going home to stay—
Meet me there.

Here our fondest hopes are vain,
Dearest links are rent in twain,
But in heav'n no throb of pain—
Meet me there;
By the river sparkling bright
In the city of delight,
Where our faith is lost in sight,
Meet me there.

Where the harps of angels ring
And the blest forever sing,
In the palace of the King,
Meet me there;
Where in sweet communion blend
Heart with heart and friend with friend,
In a world that ne'er shall end,
Meet me there.

Meet me there, Meet me there,
Where the tree of life is blooming,
Meet me there;
When the storms of life are o'er,
On the happy, golden shore,
Where the faithful part no more,
Meet me there.

Henrietta E. Blair

Dwelling in Beulah Land

Far away the noise of strife upon my ear is falling,
Then I know the sins of earth beset on ev'ry hand:

Doubt and fear and things of earth in vain to me
  are calling,
None of these shall move me from Beulah Land.

Far below the storm of doubt upon the world is beating,
Sons of men in battle long the enemy withstand:
Safe am I within the castle of God's Word retreating,
Nothing then can reach me—'tis Beulah Land.

Let the stormy breezes blow, their cry cannot alarm me;
I am safely sheltered here, protected by God's hand:
Here the sun is always shining, here there's naught can
  harm me,
I am safe forever in Beulah Land.

Viewing here the works of God, I sink in contemplation,
Hearing now His blessed voice, I see the way He planned:
Dwelling in the Spirit, here I learn of full salvation,
Gladly will I tarry in Beulah Land.

I'm living on the mountain, underneath a cloudless sky,
I'm drinking at the fountain that never shall run dry;
O yes! I'm feasting on the manna from a bountiful supply,
For I am dwelling in Beulah Land.

C. Austin Miles

The Home Over There

O think of the home over there,
By the side of the river of light,
Where the saints, all immortal and fair,
Are robed in their garments of white.

O think of the friends over there,
Who before us the journey have trod,
Of the songs that they breathe on the air,
In their home in the palace of God.

My Savior is now over there,
There my kindred and friends are at rest;
Then away from my sorrow and care,
Let me fly to the land of the blest.

I'll soon be at home over there,
For the end of my journey I see;
Many dear to my heart, over there,
Are watching and waiting for me.

Over there, over there,
O think of the home over there,
Over there, over there, over there,
O think of the home over there.

D. W. C. Huntington

Heaven Is Calling Me Home

Wonderful gladness now is filling my soul,
Heaven is calling, calling me home;
Each day I'm drawing nearer, to that bright goal,
Heaven is calling, calling me home.

Beautiful city, streets are paved with pure gold,
Heaven is calling, calling me home;
Youthful forever, none shall ever grow old,
Heaven is calling, calling me home.

I have a mansion in that blessed estate,
Heaven is calling, calling me home;
O glory, Jesus will meet me at the pearly white gate,
Heaven is calling, calling me home.

Heaven is calling, calling me home.
Heaven is calling, calling me home,
Loved ones are waiting, 'neath that bright dome;

Soon I'll go sailing o'er the mystical foam,
Heaven is calling, calling me home.

Marion W. Easterling

I'm Going Home

My heav'nly home is bright and fair;
Nor pain nor death can enter there;
Its glitt'ring tow'rs the sun outshine;
That heav'nly mansion shall be mine.

My Father's house is built on high,
Far, far above the starry sky;
When from this earthly prison free,
That heav'nly mansion mine shall be.

Let others seek a home below,
Which flames devour, or floods o'erflow,
Be mine the happier lot, to own
A heavenly mansion near the throne.

Then fail this earth, let stars decline,
And sun and moon refuse to shine;
All nature sink and cease to be,
That heavenly mansion stands for me.

I'm going home, I'm going home,
I'm going home to die no more:
To die no more, to die no more,
I'm going home to die no more.

William Hunter

Ten Thousand Times Ten Thousand

Ten thousand times ten thousand, in sparkling raiment bright,
The armies of the ransomed saints throng up the steeps of light,

'Tis finished, all is finished, their fight with death and sin,
Fling open wide the golden gates, and let the victors in.

What rush of alleluias fills all the earth and sky!
What ringing of a thousand harps bespeaks the triumph nigh!
O day, for which creation and all its tribes were made;
O joy, for all its former woes a thousandfold repaid!

O then what raptured greetings on Canaan's happy shore!
What knitting severed friendships up, where partings
    are no more!
Then eyes with joy shall sparkle that brimmed with tears of late,
Orphans no longer fatherless, nor widows desolate.

Bring near thy great salvation, thou Lamb for sinners slain;
Fill up the roll of Thine elect, then take Thy power and reign,
Appear, desire of nations, thine exiles long for home;
Show in the heavens Thy promised sign; Thou Prince
    and Savior, come.

Henry Alford

This hymn was chosen to be sung in the churchyard at the close of Alford's funeral exercises. He asked that his tombstone read, "The inn of a traveler on his way to Jerusalem." Alford was an able and eloquent preacher who served with distinction as the Dean of Canterbury. He was especially revered for his four-volume edition of the Greek Testament.

In Heaven Above

In heaven above, in heaven above,
Where God our Father dwells,
How boundless there the blessedness!
No tongue its greatness tells;

There face to face, and full and free,
Ever and evermore we see
We see the Lord of hosts!

In heaven above, in heaven above,
What glory deep and bright!
The splendor of the noonday sun
Grows pale before its light;
That mighty Sun that never goes down,
Before whose face clouds never frown,
Is God the Lord of hosts!

In heaven above, in heaven above,
No tears of pain are shed;
Here nothing ever shall fade or die;
Life's fullness around is spread,
And, like an old ocean, joy overflows,
And with immortal mercy glows,
Our God the Lord of hosts!

In heaven above, in heaven above,
God hath a joy prepared,
Which mortal ear hath never heard,
Nor mortal vision shared,
Which never entered mortal breast,
By mortal lips was never expressed,
'Tis God the Lord of hosts!

Laurenitus Laurentii Laurinus

Then I Saw a New Heaven and Earth

Then I saw a new heav'n and earth,
For the first had passed away,
And the holy city come down from God,

Like a bride on her wedding day.
And I know how He loves His own,
For I heard His great voice tell,
They would be His people, and He their God,
And among them He came to dwell.

He will wipe away every tear,
Even death shall die at last;
There'll be no more crying, or grief, or pain,
They belong to the world that's past.
And the One on the throne said "Look!
I am making all things new."
He is A and Z, He is first and last,
And His words are exact and true.

So the thirsty can drink their fill
At the fountain giving life;
But the gates are shut on all evil things,
On deceit and decay and strife.
With foundations and walls and tow'rs
Like a jewel the city shines,
With its streets of gold and its gates of pearl,
In a glory where each combines.

As they measured its length and breadth
I could see no temple there,
For its only temple is God the Lord
And the Lamb in that city fair.
And it needs neither sun nor moon
In a place which knows no night,
For the city's lamp is the Lamb Himself,
And the glory of God its light.

And I saw by the sacred throne
Flowing water, crystal clear,
And the tree of life with its healing leaves

And its fruit growing all the year.
So the worshipers of the Lamb
Bear His name, and see His face;
And they reign and serve and forever live
To the praise of His glorious grace.

Christopher M. Idle

Whose Builder and Maker Is God

I joy and rejoice that tomorrow,
When life's farthest mile I have trod,
I shall go to a home in that city,
Whose builder and maker is God.

Though here I have known but a cottage,
Though here I have passed under the rod,
Naught of this will be mine in that city,
Whose builder and maker is God.

Though life has had much to discourage,
With days but a long weary plod,
My home will have charm in that city,
Whose builder and maker is God.

Some day will these eyes close forever,
On scenes, by life's highway I have trod,
They will open again in that city,
Whose builder and maker is God.

In that city whose builder is God,
Whose builder and maker is God;
Where the Lamb is the light,
And there cometh no night,
In that city whose builder is God.

John R. Clements

At Eventide

At eventide when Christ my Lord shall call me,
And my frail bark shall sail the unknown sea,
From out the mansions of that blest eternity
A light will shed its golden beams on me.

At eventide my heart will fear no evil,
For Christ will never, never leave His own;
He'll bear my spirit o'er the silent river,
Where pain and sorrow shall no more be known.

At eventide I'll meet my loved ones yonder,
And walk with them beside the crystal sea;
With them I'll join the ransomed ones in singing
His praises through a long eternity.

At eventide there will be light, be light for me,
The light that never was on land or sea;
A light to shine to shine thro' all eternity,
At eventide there will be light, be light for me.

B. B. McKinney (1886–1952)

Not Half Has Ever Been Told

I have read of a beautiful city,
Far away in the kingdom of God;
I have read how its walls are of jasper,
How its streets are all golden and broad:
In the midst of the street is life's river,
Clear as crystal and pure to behold,
But not half of that city's bright glory
To mortals has ever been told.

I have read of bright mansions in heaven,
Which the Savior has gone to prepare;
And the saints who on earth have been faithful,

Rest forever with Christ over there;
There no sin ever enters, nor sorrow,
The inhabitants never grow old;
But not half of the wonderful story
To mortals has ever been told.

I have read of white robes for the righteous,
Of bright crowns which the glorified wear,
When our Father shall bid them "Come, enter,
And My glory eternally share,"
How the righteous are evermore blessed
As they walk thro' the streets of pure gold;
But not half of the wonderful story
To mortals has ever been told.

I have read of a Christ so forgiving,
That vile sinners may ask and receive
Peace and pardon for ev'ry transgression,
If when asking they only believe.
I have read how He'll guide and protect us,
If for safety we enter His fold;
But not half of His goodness and mercy
To mortals has ever been told.

Not half has ever been told;
Not half has ever been told;
Not half of that city's bright glory
To mortals has ever been told.

John Burch Atchinson

No Night There

In the land of fadeless day
Lies "the city foursquare,"
It shall never pass away,
And there is "no night there."

All the gates of pearl are made,
In "the city foursquare,"
All the streets with gold are laid,
And there is "no night there."

And the gates shall never close,
To "the city foursquare,"
There life's crystal river flows,
And there is "no night there."

There they need no sunshine bright,
In "that city foursquare,"
For the Lamb is all the light,
And there is "no night there."

God shall "wipe away all tears";
There's no death, no pain, nor fears;
And they count not time by years,
For there is "no night there."

John R. Clements

No Disappointment in Heaven

There's no disappointment in heaven,
No weariness, sorrow or pain;
No hearts that are bleeding and broken,
No song with a minor refrain.
The clouds of our earthly horizon
Will never appear in the sky,
For all will be sunshine and gladness,
With never a sob nor a sigh.

We'll never pay rent for our mansion,
The taxes will never come due;
Our garments will never grow threadbare,
But always be fadeless and new.

We'll never be hungry nor thirsty,
Nor languish in poverty there,
For all the rich bounties of heaven
His sanctified children will share.

There'll never be crepe on the door-knob,
No funeral train in the sky;
No graves on the hillsides of glory,
For there we shall nevermore die.
The old will be young there forever,
Transformed in a moment of time;
Immortal we'll stand in His likeness,
The stars and the sun to outshine.

I'm bound for that beautiful city
My Lord has prepared for His own;
Where all the redeemed of all ages
Sing "Glory!" around the white throne;
Sometimes I grow homesick for heaven,
And the glories I there shall behold:
What a joy that will be when my Savior I see,
In that beautiful city of gold!

F. M. Lehman

I Want to Go There

They tell of a city far up in the sky,
I want to go there, I do;
'Tis built in the land of "the sweet by and by,"
I want to go there, don't you?
There Jesus has gone to prepare us a home,
I want to go there, I do;
Where sickness nor sorrow nor death ever come,
I want to go there, don't you?

Its gates are all pearl, its streets are all gold,
I want to go there, I do;
The Lamb is the light of that city, we're told,
I want to go there, don't you?
Death robs us all here, there none ever die,
I want to go there, I do;
Where loved ones will never again say goodbye,
I want to go there, don't you?

When the old ship of Zion shall make her last trip,
I want to be there, I do;
With heads all uncovered to greet the old ship,
I want to be there, don't you?
When all the ship's company meet on the strand,
I want to be there, I do;
"With songs on our lips and with harps in our hands,"
I want to be there, don't you?

When Jesus is crowned the King of all kings,
I want to be there, I do;
With shouting and clapping till all heaven rings,
I want to be there, don't you?
Hallelujah! we'll shout again and again,
I want to be there, I do;
And close with the chorus, Amen, and Amen,
I want to be there, don't you?

I want to go there, I want to go there,
I want to go there, I do;
I want to go there, I want to go there,
I want to go there, don't you?

Rev. D. Sullins

Gathering Home

Up to the bountiful Giver of life,
Gathering home! gathering home!
Up to the dwelling where cometh no strife,
The dear ones are gathering home.

Up to the city where falleth no light,
Gathering home! gathering home!
Up where the Savior's own face is the light,
The dear ones are gathering home.

Up to the beautiful mansions above,
Gathering home! gathering home!
Safe in the arms of His infinite love,
The dear ones are gathering home.

Gathering home! gathering home!
Never to sorrow more, never to roam;
Gathering home! gathering home!
God's children are gathering home!

Mrs. Mariana B. Slade

Rest for the Weary

In the Christian's home in glory,
There remains a land of rest;
There my Savior's gone before me,
To fulfill my soul's request.

He is fitting up my mansion,
Which eternally shall stand,
For my stay shall not be transient,
In that holy, happy land.

Pain and sickness ne'er shall enter,
Grief nor woe my lot shall share;
But, in that celestial center,
I a crown of life shall wear.

Death itself shall then be vanquished,
And his sting shall be withdrawn;
Shall for gladness, oh, ye ransomed!
Hail with joy the rising morn.

There is rest for the weary,
There is rest for the weary,
There is rest for the weary,
There is rest for you.

On the other side of Jordan,
In the sweet fields of Eden,
Where the tree of life is blooming,
There is rest for you.

William Hunter

The Father's House

No, not cold beneath the grasses,
Nor close-walled within the tomb;
Rather, in our Father's mansion,
Living in another room.

Living like the one who loves me,
Like my child with cheek abloom,
Out of sight, at desk or school-book,
Busy in another room.

Nearer is my love, whom fortune
Beckons where the strange lands loom;

Just behind the hanging curtains,
Serving in another room.

Shall I doubt my Father's mercy?
Shall I think of death as doom?
Or the stepping o'er the threshold
To a bigger, brighter room?

Shall I blame my Father's wisdom?
Shall I sit enswathed in gloom?
When I know my loves are happy,
Waiting in another room.

Robert Freeman

"In my Father's house are many mansions" (John 14:2).

Someday, We Shall Understand

Not now, but in the coming years,
*   It may be in the better land,*
We'll read the meaning of our tears,
*   And there, someday, we'll understand.*

We'll catch the broken threads again
*   And finish what here we began;*
Heaven shall the mysteries explain,
*   And then, ah then, we'll understand.*

God knows the way, He holds the key.
*   He guides us with unerring hand;*
Sometime, with tearless eyes, we'll see;
*   Yes there, up there, we'll understand,*

Then trust in God through all thy days.
*   Fear not, for He doth hold thy hand.*

Though dark the way, still sing and pray;
Sometime, someday, we'll understand.

El Nathan

"Jesus answered and said unto him, What I do thou knowest not now, but thou shalt know hereafter" (John 13:7).

"For now we see through a glass darkly; but then face to face: now I know in part; but then shall I know even as also I am known" (1 Cor. 13:12).

The Loom of Time

Man's life is laid in the loom of time
To a pattern he does not see,
While the weavers work and the shuttles fly
Till the dawn of eternity.

Some shuttles are filled with silver threads
And some with threads of gold,
While often but the darker hues
Are all that they may hold.

But the weaver watches with skillful eye
Each shuttle fly to and fro,
And sees the pattern so deftly wrought
As the loom moves sure and slow.

God surely planned the pattern.
Each thread, the dark and fair,
Is chosen by His master skill
And placed in the web with care.

He only knows its beauty,
And guides the shuttles which hold

The threads so unattractive,
  As well as the threads of gold.

Not till each loom is silent,
  And the shuttles cease to fly,
Shall God reveal the pattern
  And explain the reason why.

The dark threads were as needful
  In the weaver's skillful hand
As the threads of gold and silver
  For the pattern which He planned.

Author Unknown

"For I will show him how great things he must suffer for my name's sake" (Acts 9:16).

The Children Up in Heaven

"Oh, what do you think the angels say?"
  Said the children up in heaven;
"There's a dear little girl coming home today,
She's almost ready to fly away
From the earth where we used to live.
Let's go and open the gates of pearl,
Open them wide for a new little girl,"
  Said the children up in heaven.

"God wanted her here where His little ones meet,"
  Said the children up in heaven;
"She will play with us in the golden street:
She has grown too fair, she has grown too sweet,
For the earth where we used to live.
She needed the sunshine, this dear little girl,

That gilds this side of the gates of pearl,"
  Said the children up in heaven.

"Fly with her quickly, O angels dear,"
  Said the children up in heaven.
"See—she is coming. Look there
At the jasper light in her sunny hair."
Ah, hush, hush! All the swift wings furl!
For the King Himself, at the gates of pearl,
Is taking her hand, my sweet little girl,
  And is leading her into heaven.

Edith Gilling Cherry

"But Jesus said, Suffer little children, and forbid them not,
to come unto me: for of such is the kingdom of heaven"
(Matt. 19:14).

Afraid?

To feel the spirit's glad release?
To pass from pain to perfect peace,
The strife and strain of life to cease?
  Afraid—of that?

Afraid to see the Savior's face,
To hear His welcome and to trace
The glory gleam from wounds of grace?
  Afraid? Of what?

A flash, a crash, a pierced heart,
Darkness, light, O heaven's art!
A wound of His a counterpart!
  Afraid? Of that?

To do by death what life could not,
Baptize with blood a stony plot,

Till souls shall blossom from the spot—
  Afraid—of THAT?

C. H. Hamilton

"For to me to live is Christ, and to die is gain . . . having a desire to depart, and to be with Christ; which is far better" (Phil. 1:21, 23).

This poem was written by a missionary in Kiangsu, after the martyrdom of missionary J. W. Vinson in China. It was the favorite poem of the martyrs John and Betty Stam.

Peace

With eager heart and will and fire
I fought to win my great desire;
"Peace shall be mine," I said, but life
Grew bitter in the endless strife.

My soul was weary, and my pride
Was wounded deep; to heaven I cried,
"God grant me peace or I must die!"
The dumb stars glittered no reply.

Broken at last I bowed my head,
Forgetting all myself, and said,
"Whatever comes, His will be done."
And in that moment peace was won.

Henry Van Dyke

"Father, if thou be willing, remove this cup from me; nevertheless not my will, but thine, be done" (Luke 22:42).

The Christian's Good-night

Sleep on, beloved, sleep, and take thy rest;
Lay down thy head upon thy Saviour's breast;
We love thee well, but Jesus loves thee best—
Good-night!

Calm is thy slumber as an infant's sleep;
But thou shalt take no more to toil and weep;
Thine is a perfect rest secure and deep—
Good-night!

Until the shadows of this earth are cast;
Until He gathers in His sheaves at last;
Until the twilight gloom be overpast—
Good-night!

Until the Easter glory lights the skies;
Until the dead in Jesus shall arise;
And He shall come, but not in lowly guise—
Good-night!

Until, made beautiful by Love Divine,
Thou, in the likeness of thy Lord shall shine,
And He shall bring that golden crown of thine—
Good-night!

Only "Good-night," beloved, not "Farewell";
A little while and all His saints shall dwell
In hallowed union indivisible—
Good-night!

Until we meet again before His throne,
Clothed in the spotless robe He gives His own,
Until we know even as we are known—
Good-night!

Sarah Doudney

"Our friend Lazarus sleepeth, but I go, that I may awake him out of sleep" (John 11:11).

"And when he had said this, he fell asleep" (Acts 7:60).

This hymn was sung by Ira D. Sankey at the funeral service for the world-renowned nineteenth-century British preacher Charles Haddon Spurgeon.

What Is Life?

What is life? 'tis but a vapor;
  Soon it vanishes away.
Life is but a dying taper—
  O, my soul, why wish to stay!
Why not spread thy wings and fly
  Straight to yonder world of joy.

See that glory, how resplendent!
  Brighter far than fancy paints;
There, in majesty transcendent,
  Jesus reigns the King of saints.
Why not spread, thy wings and fly
  Straight to yonder world of joy.

Joyful crowds, His throne surrounding,
  Sing with rapture of His love;
Through the heavens His praise resounding,
  Filling all the courts above.
Why not spread thy wings and fly
  Straight to yonder world of joy.

T. Hastings

Safely Home

I am home in Heaven, dear ones;
  All's so happy, all's so bright!
There's perfect joy and beauty
  In this everlasting light.

All the pain and grief are over,
  Every restless tossing passed;
I am now at peace forever,
  Safely home in Heaven at last.

Did you wonder I so calmly
  Trod the Valley of the shade?
Oh! but Jesus' love illumined
  Every dark and fearful glade.

And He came Himself to meet me
  In that way so hard to tread;
And with Jesus' arm to lean on,
  Could I have one doubt or dread?

Then you must not grieve so sorely,
  For I love you dearly still;
Try to look beyond earth's shadows,
  Pray to trust our Father's will.

There is work still waiting for you,
  So you must not idle stand;
Do your work while life remaineth—
  You shall rest in Jesus' land.

When that work is all completed,
  He will gently call you home;
Oh, the rapture of the meeting!
  Oh, the joy to see you come!

Author Unknown

I Never Saw a Moor

I never saw a moor,
I never saw the sea;
Yet know I how the heather looks,
And what a wave must be.

I never spoke with God,
Nor visited in Heaven;
Yet certain am I of the spot
As if the chart were given.

Emily Dickinson

This American poet found words to express her own belief in the heavenly abode.

Prospice

Fear death?—to feel the fog in my throat,
The mist in my face,
When the snows begin, and the blasts denote
I am nearing the place,
The power of the night, the press of the storm,
The post of the foe;
Where he stands, the Arch Fear in a visible form,
Yet the strong man must go:
For the journey is done and the summit attained,
And the barriers fall,
Though a battle's to fight ere the guerdon be gained,
The reward of it all.
I was ever a fighter, so—one fight more,
The best and the last!
I would hate that death bandaged my eyes, and forbore,
And bade me creep past.

No! let me taste the whole of it, fare like my peers
   The heroes of old,
Bear the brunt, in a minute pay glad life's arrears
   Of pain, darkness and cold.
For sudden the worse turns the best to the brave,
   The black minute's at end,
And the elements' rage, the fiend-voices that rave,
   Shall dwindle, shall blend,
Shall change, shall become first a peace out of pain,
   Then a light, then thy breast,
O thou soul of my soul! I shall clasp thee again,
   And with God be the rest!

Robert Browning

Few poets exhibited the spiritual sensitivities of Robert Browning. Despite the sorrows and tragedies which plagued him, he never lost his hope for eternal rest.

Epilogue

One who never turned his back but marched breast forward,
   Never doubted clouds would break,
Never dreamed, though right were worsted, wrong
      would triumph,
Held we fall to rise, are baffled to fight better,
   Sleep to wake.

Robert Browning

At the end of his life, Robert Browning wrote "Epilogue" and asked that it conclude all his published works as a testimony to his faith.

The Things in the Cabinet Drawer

There are whips and tops and pieces of string
And shoes that no little feet ever wear;
There are bits of ribbon and broken wings
And tresses of golden hair.

There are dainty jackets that never are worn
There are toys and models of ships;
There are books and pictures all faded and torn
And marked by finger tips
Of dimpled hands that have fallen to dust—
Yet we strive to think that the Lord is just.

Yet a feeling of bitterness fills our soul;
Sometimes we try to pray,
That the Reaper has spared so many flowers
And taken ours away.
And we sometimes doubt if the Lord can know
How our riven hearts did love them so.

But we think of our dear ones dead,
Our children who never grow old,
And how they are waiting and watching for us
In the city with streets of gold;
And how they are safe through all the years
From sickness and want and war.
We thank the great God, with falling tears,
For the things in the cabinet drawer.

Anonymous

There is perhaps no hurt any deeper nor any sorrow any
heavier to bear than the loss of a child. Only the blessed
Savior can bring comfort now and hope for a future reunion.

I'm a Pilgrim

I'm a pilgrim, and I'm a stranger;
I can tarry, I can tarry but a night!
Do not detain me, for I am going
To where the streamlets are ever flowing.

Of that city, to which I journey;
My Redeemer, my Redeemer is the light;
There is no sorrow, nor any sighing,
Nor any tears there, nor any dying:

There the sunbeams are ever shining,
Oh, my longing heart, my longing heart is there;
Here in this country, so dark and dreary,
I long have wander'd forlorn and weary.

Author Unknown

Crossing the Bar

Sunset and evening star,
And one clear call for me!
And may there be no moaning of the bar
When I put out to sea,

But such a tide as moving seems asleep,
Too full for sound and foam,
When that which drew from out the boundless deep
Turns again home.

Twilight and evening bell,
And after that the dark!
And may there be no sadness of farewell
When I embark;

For, though from out our bourne of time and place
The flood may bear me far,
I hope to see my Pilot face to face
When I have crossed the bar.

Alfred Tennyson, 1889

This God-fearing poet requested that "Crossing the Bar" be printed at the conclusion of each volume of his published works. Its words expressed vividly the hope which beat within his breast.

A Boy Meets God

Look God: I have never spoken to You,
But now I want to say, "How do You do."
You see God, they told me You did not exist;
And, like a fool, I believed all of this.
Last night from a shell hole I saw Your sky;
I figured right then they had told me a lie.
Had I taken the time to see the things You made,
I would know they weren't calling a spade a spade.
I wonder, God, if You would shake my hand;
Somehow, I feel that You will understand.
Strange, I had to come to this hellish place
Before I had time to see Your face.
Well, I guess there isn't much more to say,
But I am sure glad, God, I met You today.
I guess the zero hour will soon be here,
But I am not afraid since I know You are near.
The signal—well, God, I will have to go;
I love you lots, this I want you to know.
Looks like this will be a horrible fight;
Who knows, I may come to your house tonight.

Though I wasn't friendly with you before,
I wonder, God, if you would wait at the door.
Look, I am crying, me shedding tears!
I wish I had known you these many years.
Well, I will have to go now, God. Goodbye—
Strange, since I met you, I am not afraid to die.

Author Unknown

This poem was found on the body of a nineteen-year-old American soldier in Vietnam.

With Our Sympathy

After the tempest—calm,
After the shadow—light,
And the golden dawn breaks clearly.
After the long, long night,
After the rain, the sunshine,
After the tears, the laughter—
    And when this life is over,
    Life eternal follows after.

Author unknown

The Homeland

    Think
Of stepping on shore
    and finding it
    Heaven!

Of taking hold of a hand
    and finding it
    God's hand!

232

Of breathing a new air
  and finding it
  celestial air!

Of feeling invigorated
  and finding it
  immortality!

Of passing
  from storm and tempest,
  to an unbroken calm!

Of waking up
  and finding
  yourself
  HOME!

HALLELUJAH!

This anonymous poem was uncovered by Ruth Ray Hunt. Ruth was so moved by its beauty and message that she passed the words on to her pastor, Dr. Criswell. These words were later framed by Don Wyrtzen in the beautiful melody which was to be wafted throughout the land to comfort and inspire through the song "Finally Home."